SOUND INNOVATIONS

ENSEMBLE DEVELOPMENT

Chorales and Warm-up Exercises for Tone, Technique and Rhythm

INTERMEDIATE CONCERT BAND

Peter **BOONSHAFT** | Chris **BERNOTAS**

Thank you for making *Sound Innovations: Ensemble Development* a part of your concert band curriculum. With 412 exercises, including over 70 chorales by some of today's most renowned composers for concert band, it is our hope you will find this book to be a valuable resource in helping your students grow in their understanding and abilities as an ensemble musician.

The exercises are grouped by key and presented in a variety of intermediate difficulty levels. Where possible, several exercises in the same category are provided to allow for variety while accomplishing the goals of that specific type of exercise. You will notice that many exercises and chorales are clearly marked with dynamics, articulations, style and tempo for students to practice those aspects of performance. Other exercises are intentionally left for the teacher to determine how best to use them in facilitating the goals and addressing the needs of their ensemble.

Whether your students are progressing through exercises to better their technical facility or challenging their musicianship with beautiful chorales, we are confident your concert band performers will be excited, motivated and inspired by using *Sound Innovations: Ensemble Development*.

Alfred Music
P.O. Box 10003
Van Nuys, CA 91410-0003
alfred.com

ISBN-10: 0-7390-6765-6
ISBN-13: 978-0-7390-6765-9

Instrument photos courtesy of Yamaha Corporation of America Band & Orchestral Division

Contents

Passing the Tonic

These exercises offer students the opportunity to concentrate on improving their individual characteristic tone and tuning skills as they work to achieve ensemble balance, blend and intonation. Each line is designed to help students become accustomed to the tonality of the key, develop a cohesive ensemble sound, and work toward stabilizing the pitch as they move the tonic note through various sections of the band. For minor keys, there are triads included so students can hear the minor tonality.

Breathing and Long Tones

Teachers may use these exercises to foster deep, full breaths using a variety of approaches and techniques such as exhalation, metered breathing or quick, intense breaths. Through the use of long tones, interspersed with humming and/or singing, students can focus on improving air capacity, breath support, resistance and tone quality, as well as the essential ability to internalize pitch.

Major Scale

Students can work toward mastering the major scale for the key in its most common rhythmic form.

Natural Minor Scale

Students can work toward mastering the natural minor scale for the key in its most common rhythmic form.

Harmonic and Melodic Minor Scales

Students can work toward mastering the harmonic and melodic forms of the minor scale for the key in its most common rhythmic form.

Scale Pattern

These exercises are designed to give students the opportunity to develop their dexterity, facility, confidence and familiarity with the scale of the key using a number of different patterns, each providing a variety of rhythms, meters and articulations.

Changing Scale Rhythm

Through these exercises, students can practice playing the scale for the key in a challenging and unpredictable rhythmic context.

Chromatic Scale

A chromatic scale, starting on the tonic of the key is provided for students to develop technical proficiency and facility.

Flexibility

Flexibility exercises are intended to help students reinforce good embouchure habits and muscle development, as well as breath support, intensity of airstream and intonation.

Arpeggios

Various patterns of arpeggios are included to help students develop technical proficiency, as well as explore melodic and harmonic aspects in each key.

Intervals

A variety of interval studies are presented to aid students in developing their technique, intonation and tone quality, as well as their ability to internalizing pitch.

Balance and Intonation: Perfect Intervals

In these exercises, the ensemble begins by playing in unison, before some of the players move to create a perfect fifth, before returning to the starting unison pitch. Following this pattern, students will have the opportunity to focus on tuning the perfect intervals of a unison, fourth, fifth and octave.

Balance and Intonation: Diatonic Harmony

By having students move between perfect intervals and diatonic triads, these exercises will foster the skills of vertical and horizontal tuning, balance, blend and internalizing pitch. These exercises will also help students better understand common cadences and harmonic progressions.

Balance and Intonation: Family Balance

Family Balance exercises are designed to focus on various aspects of ensemble, family and section balance, as well as intonation, pitch tendencies, listening and blending.

Balance and Intonation: Layered Tuning

In these exercises, intervals and triads are built by gradually adding one member of an interval or triad at a time, allowing students to focus on tuning vertical sonorities in a variety of contexts. With a similar focus, students will also gradually subtract members of vertical sonorities one member at a time.

Balance and Intonation: Moving Chord Tones

These exercises begin with each part playing one of the three notes of a triad. Subsequent measures have each part cycle through the other two members of that triad, before arriving back to the original pitch. The goal is for each presentation of the triad to be performed equally well in tune as students practice playing the various members of a triad.

Balance and Intonation: Shifting Chord Qualities

These exercises begin with the ensemble playing a major triad. In measure 2, the third of the triad moves downward a half-step to create a minor triad. In measure 3, the fifth of the triad moves downward a half-step to create a diminished triad. Finally, measure 4 has the root of the triad move downward a half-step to create a major triad. Cycling through these chord qualities will help foster horizontal and vertical tuning, as well as balance, blend and internalizing pitch.

Expanding Intervals

From their starting pitch, students move to a pitch one half-step away before returning back to the original pitch. Following that pattern, they gradually increase the distance of that interval by a half step each time. These exercises are presented with the expanding intervals moving downward and moving upward, as well as in parallel octaves, fifths and thirds. These exercises offer a wonderful opportunity to develop the skills of tuning horizontally as well as vertically while attending to balance, blend and intonation.

Rhythm

These exercises focus on various aspects of rhythm and meter, providing material that will allow students to practice, review and challenge their skills. They also provide excellent practice in sight-reading.

Rhythmic Subdivision

These exercises are designed to help students understand and internalize rhythmic subdivision. While one part of the ensemble performs music containing common rhythmic patterns, the other part of the ensemble performs a supporting line that includes the playing of the subdivision required for the first line to be played correctly.

Meter

Students can explore these new meters in straightforward exercises designed to introduce them with limited rhythmic challenges.

Phrasing

These exercises provide students an opportunity to develop their sense of individual and ensemble phrasing. Students will practice where they should breathe as well as where they should not breathe in a variety of musical examples. Each exercise can be used to focus on the subtleties of musical releases, phrase lengths, contour of line and shaping of phrases in various contexts.

Articulation

These exercises allow students to practice performing, controlling, changing and contrasting a variety of articulations in many contexts.

Dynamics

Through these exercises, students will have the opportunity to further develop their abilities to perform and control dynamic levels while practicing sudden changes, gradual changes, extremes and nuances of volume.

Etude

These short studies reinforce various aspects of individual and ensemble performance while providing the challenge of combining those concepts in a variety of ways.

Scale Chorale

These chorales are harmonized scales of that key. Each student's part has two lines: the scale (the top line, A), and their part in the chorale (the bottom line, B). Directors can choose a single student, a section, a family, or any other combination of instrumentalists to play the scale while the rest of the ensemble plays the chorale setting.

Chorale

A variety of chorales, written by some of the finest composers of music for young band, provide opportunities for students to develop the essential skills of tone production, blend, balance, intonation, phrasing, dynamics, articulation, style and musical expression.

Advancing Rhythm and Meter

This section of the book provides students exercises using more challenging rhythms and meters. Advanced rhythmic patterns in $\frac{6}{8}$ meter, advanced eighth-note triplet patterns, and quarter-note triplets are explored. Also included are basic presentations of $\frac{3}{8}$, $\frac{9}{8}$, $\frac{12}{8}$, $\frac{5}{8}$ and $\frac{7}{8}$ meter. In addition, examples of changing meter from $\frac{4}{4}$ to $\frac{6}{8}$ and $\frac{3}{4}$ to $\frac{6}{8}$ are included.

Keys Included

Though the following keys are introduced, there is special emphasis on the keys most common in intermediate band literature. Keys are introduced in the following order: concert Bb major, G minor, Eb major, C minor, F major, D minor, Ab major, F minor, Db major, Bb minor, C major, A minor, G major and E minor.

Percussion

Percussion parts are provided for battery instruments, accessories, mallets and timpani, offering the percussion section an opportunity to perform as members of the ensemble with parts integrated into every exercise in the book.

Sound Innovations:
Ensemble Development Rudiments

- Single Stroke Roll
- Single Stroke 4 /Four Stroke Ruff
- Single Stroke 7
- Multiple Bounce Roll
- Double Stroke Open Roll
- 5-Stroke Roll
- 7-Stroke Roll
- 9-Stroke Roll
- 13-Stroke Roll
- 17-Stroke Roll
- Single Paradiddle
- Double Paradiddle

- Triple Paradiddle
- Flam
- Flam Accent
- Flam Tap
- Flamacue
- Flam Paradiddle
- Drag
- Single Drag Tap
- Lesson 25
- Drag Paradiddle #1
- Single Ratamacue

Percussion 2 Instruments Included and Their Abbreviations

- Woodblock (W.B.)
- Cowbell (C.B.)
- Tambourine (Tamb.)
- Suspended Cymbal (Sus. Cym.)
- Crash Cymbals (Cr. Cym.)
- China Cymbal
- Triangle (Tri.)
- Temple Blocks

- Finger Cymbals
- Sleigh Bells
- Mark Tree
- Cabasa
- Claves
- Concert Tom(s)
- Bongos
- Tam-Tam/Gong

Table of Contents

Title	Conductor Page	Student Page

Concert B♭ Major

1. Passing the Tonic	9	2
2. Passing the Tonic	10	2
3. Passing the Tonic	11	2
4. Passing the Tonic	12	2
5. Passing the Tonic	13	2
6. Breathing and Long Tones	14	2
7. Breathing and Long Tones	15	2
8. Breathing and Long Tones	16	2
9. Breathing and Long Tones	17	2
10. Major Scale	18	3
11. Scale Pattern	19	3
12. Scale Pattern	20	3
13. Scale Pattern	21	3
14. Scale Pattern	22	3
15. Scale Pattern	24	3
16. Changing Scale Rhythm	26	3
17. Chromatic Scale	27	3
18. Flexibility	28	4
19. Flexibility	29	4
20. Arpeggios	30	4
21. Arpeggios	31	4
22. Intervals	32	4
23. Intervals	33	4
24. Balance and Intonation: Perfect Intervals	34	4
25. Balance and Intonation: Diatonic Harmony	35	4
26. Balance and Intonation: Family Balance	36	4
27. Balance and Intonation: Layered Tuning	37	5
28. Balance and Intonation: Moving Chord Tones	38	5
29. Balance and Intonation: Shifting Chord Qualities	39	5
30. Expanding Intervals: Downward in Parallel Octaves	40	5
31. Expanding Intervals: Downward in Parallel Fifths	41	5
32. Expanding Intervals: Downward in Triads	42	5
33. Expanding Intervals: Upward in Parallel Octaves	43	5
34. Expanding Intervals: Upward in Triads	44	5
35. Rhythm	45	5
36. Rhythm	46	6
37. Rhythm	47	6
38. Rhythm	48	6
39. Rhythm	49	6
40. Rhythmic Subdivision	50	6
41. Rhythmic Subdivision	52	6
42. Rhythmic Subdivision	54	6
43. Meter	56	6
44. Phrasing	57	7
45. Phrasing	58	7
46. Articulation	59	7
47. Dynamics	60	7
48. Etude	61	7
49. Etude	64	7
50. Chorale: Jesu, meine Zuversicht arranged by Todd Stalter	67	8
51. Chorale by Michael Story	68	8
52A. and 52B. Scale Chorale by Chris M. Bernotas	69	8
53. Chorale by Chris M. Bernotas	70	8
54. Chorale by Randall D. Standridge	71	8
55. Chorale by Andrew Boysen, Jr.	73	8
56. Chorale by Ralph Ford	76	9
57. Chorale by Robert Sheldon	77	9
58. Chorale by Roland Barrett	79	9
59. Chorale by Chris M. Bernotas	82	9
60. Chorale by Rossano Galante	84	9

Concert G Minor

61. Passing the Tonic	86	10
62. Breathing and Long Tones	87	10
63. Natural Minor Scale	88	10
64. Harmonic and Melodic Minor Scales	89	10
65. Scale Pattern	90	10
66. Chromatic Scale	91	10
67. Flexibility	92	10
68. Flexibility	93	10
69. Arpeggios	94	10
70. Arpeggios	95	11
71. Intervals	96	11
72. Intervals	97	11
73. Balance and Intonation: Diatonic Harmony	98	11
74. Balance and Intonation: Moving Chord Tones	99	11
75. Balance and Intonation: Layered Tuning	100	11
76. Balance and Intonation: Family Balance	101	11
77. Expanding Intervals: Downward in Parallel Fifths	102	11
78. Expanding Intervals: Upward in Parallel Thirds	103	11
79. Rhythm	104	12
80. Rhythm	105	12
81. Rhythm	106	12
82. Rhythmic Subdivision	107	12
83. Rhythmic Subdivision	109	12
84. Articulation and Dynamics	111	12
85. Etude	112	12
86. Chorale by Robert Sheldon	114	13
87. Chorale by Michael Story	115	13
88A. & 88B. Scale Chorale by Chris M. Bernotas	116	13
89. Chorale by Andrew Boysen, Jr.	117	13
90. Chorale by Rossano Galante	120	13

Concert E♭ Major

91. Passing the Tonic	122	14
92. Passing the Tonic	123	14
93. Passing the Tonic	124	14
94. Passing the Tonic	125	14
95. Passing the Tonic	126	14
96. Breathing and Long Tones	127	14
97. Breathing and Long Tones	128	14
98. Breathing and Long Tones	129	14
99. Breathing and Long Tones	130	14
100. Major Scale	131	15
101. Scale Pattern	132	15
102. Scale Pattern	133	15
103. Scale Pattern	134	15
104. Scale Pattern	135	15
105. Scale Pattern	137	15

6

106. Changing Scale Rhythm 138 15
107. Chromatic Scale 139 15
108. Flexibility 140 16
109. Flexibility 141 16
110. Arpeggios 142 16
111. Arpeggios 143 16
112. Intervals 144 16
113. Intervals 145 16
114. Balance and Intonation: Perfect Intervals 146 16
115. Balance and Intonation: Diatonic Harmony 147 16
116. Balance and Intonation: Family Balance 148 16
117. Balance and Intonation: Layered Tuning 149 17
118. Balance and Intonation: Layered Tuning 150 17
119. Balance and Intonation: Shifting Chord Qualities 151 17
120. Expanding Intervals: Downward in Parallel Octaves 152 17
121. Expanding Intervals: Downward in Parallel Fifths 153 17
122. Expanding Intervals: Downward in Triads 154 17
123. Expanding Intervals: Upward in Parallel Octaves 155 17
124. Expanding Intervals: Upward in Triads 156 17
125. Rhythm 157 18
126. Rhythm 158 18
127. Rhythm 159 18
128. Rhythm 160 18
129. Rhythm 161 18
130. Rhythmic Subdivision 162 18
131. Rhythmic Subdivision 164 18
132. Rhythmic Subdivision 166 18
133. Meter 169 19
134. Phrasing 170 19
135. Phrasing 171 19
136. Articulation 172 19
137. Dynamics 173 19
138. Etude 174 19
139. Etude 176 19
140. Chorale by Todd Stalter 179 20
141. Chorale by Randall D. Standridge 181 20
142A. & 142B. Scale Chorale by Chris M. Bernotas 182 20
143. Chorale by Michael Story 183 20
144. Chorale by Andrew Boysen, Jr. 186 20
145. Chorale by Robert Sheldon 188 21
146. Chorale by Ralph Ford 190 21
147. Chorale by Rossano Galante 192 21
148. Chorale by Chris M. Bernotas 194 21
149. Chorale by Randall D. Standridge 196 21

Concert C Minor

150. Passing the Tonic 198 22
151. Breathing and Long Tones 199 22
152. Natural Minor Scale 200 22
153. Harmonic and Melodic Minor Scales 201 22
154. Scale Pattern 202 22
155. Chromatic Scale 204 22
156. Flexibility 205 22
157. Flexibility 206 22
158. Arpeggios 207 23
159. Arpeggios 208 23
160. Intervals 209 23
161. Intervals 210 23
162. Balance and Intonation: Diatonic Harmony 211 23
163. Balance and Intonation: Moving Chord Tones 212 23
164. Balance and Intonation: Layered Tuning 213 23
165. Balance and Intonation: Family Balance 214 23
166. Expanding Intervals: Downward in Triads 215 23
167. Expanding Intervals: Upward in Triads 216 23
168. Rhythm 217 24
169. Rhythm 218 24
170. Rhythm 219 24
171. Rhythmic Subdivision 220 24
172. Rhythmic Subdivision 222 24
173. Articulation and Dynamics 224 24
174. Etude 225 24
175. Chorale by Randall D. Standridge 227 25
176. Chorale by Roland Barrett 228 25
177A. & 177B. Scale Chorale by Chris M. Bernotas 230 25
178. Chorale: Meines Lebens letzte Zeit
arranged by Todd Stalter 231 25
179. Chorale by Rossano Galante 234 25

Concert F Major

180. Passing the Tonic 236 26
181. Breathing and Long Tones 237 26
182. Major Scale 238 26
183. Scale Pattern 239 26
184. Scale Pattern 241 26
185. Chromatic Scale 243 26
186. Flexibility 244 26
187. Flexibility 245 26
188. Arpeggios 246 27
189. Arpeggios 247 27
190. Intervals 248 27
191. Balance and Intonation: Diatonic Harmony 249 27
192. Balance and Intonation: Family Balance 250 27
193. Balance and Intonation: Layered Tuning 251 27
194. Balance and Intonation: Moving Chord Tones 252 27
195. Balance and Intonation: Shifting Chord Qualities 253 27
196. Expanding Intervals: Downward in Parallel Fifths 254 27
197. Expanding Intervals: Upward in Parallel Fifths 255 27
198. Rhythm 256 28
199. Rhythm 257 28
200. Rhythm 258 28
201. Rhythmic Subdivision 259 28
202. Rhythmic Subdivision 261 28
203. Articulation and Dynamics 263 28
204. Etude 264 28
205. Chorale: Overture 1812 arranged by Michael Story 267 29
206. Chorale by Randall D. Standridge 268 29
207A. & 207B. Scale Chorale by Chris M. Bernotas 270 29
208. Chorale by Rossano Galante 271 29
209. Chorale by Ralph Ford 274 29

Concert D Minor

210. Passing the Tonic 276 30
211. Breathing and Long Tones 277 30
212. Natural Minor Scale 278 30
213. Harmonic and Melodic Minor Scales 279 30
214. Scale Pattern 280 30
215. Scale Pattern 281 30
216. Chromatic Scale 283 30

217. Flexibility 284 30
218. Flexibility 285 31
219. Arpeggios 286 31
220. Arpeggios 287 31
221. Intrevals 288 31
222. Balance and Intonation: Diatonic Harmony 289 31
223. Balance and Intonation: Family Balance. 290 31
224. Balance and Intonation: Layered Tuning. 291 31
225. Balance and Intonation: Moving Chord Tones. 292 31
226. Expanding Intervals: Downward in Triads. 293 31
227. Expanding Intervals: Upward in Triads. 294 31
228. Rhythm. 295 32
229. Rhythm. 296 32
230. Rhythm. 297 32
231. Rhythmic Subdivision. 298 32
232. Rhythmic Subdivision. 300 32
233. Articulation and Dynamics 302 32
234. Etude 303 32
235. Chorale by Roland Barrett. 306 33
236. Chorale by Andrew Boysen, Jr. 308 33
237A. & 237B. Scale Chorale by Chris M. Bernotas. 309 33
238. Chorale by Robert Sheldon 310 33
239. Chorale: Psalm 33 arranged by Todd Stalter. 312 33

Concert A♭ Major

240. Passing the Tonic 315 34
241. Breathing and Long Tones. 316 34
242. Major Scale 317 34
243. Scale Pattern. 318 34
244. Scale Pattern 320 34
245. Chromatic Scale. 322 34
246. Flexibility 323 34
247. Flexibility 324 34
248. Arpeggios 325 35
249. Arpeggios 326 35
250. Intervals 327 35
251. Balance and Intonation: Diatonic Harmony 328 35
252. Balance and Intonation: Family Balance. 329 35
253. Balance and Intonation: Layered Tuning. 330 35
254. Balance and Intonation: Moving Chord Tones. 331 35
255. Expanding Intervals: Downward in Parallel Fifths 332 35
256. Expanding Intervals: Upward in Parallel Thirds 333 35
257. Rhythm. 334 36
258. Rhythm. 336 36
259. Rhythm. 337 36
260. Rhythmic Subdivision. 338 36
261. Rhythmic Subdivision. 340 36
262. Dynamics. 342 36
263. Articulation and Dynamics 343 36
264. Etude 344 36
265. Chorale by Randall D. Standridge 346 37
266. Chorale by Andrew Boysen, Jr. 348 37
267A. & 267B. Scale Chorale by Chris M. Bernotas. 350 37
268. Chorale by Ralph Ford 351 37
269. Chorale by Roland Barrett. 353 37

Concert F Minor

270. Passing the Tone. 356 38
271. Breathing and Long Tones. 357 38
272. Natural Minor Scale 358 38
273. Harmonic and Melodic Minor Scales 359 38
274. Scale Pattern. 360 38
275. Chromatic Scale. 362 38
276. Flexibility. 363 38
277. Flexibility. 364 38
278. Arpeggios 365 38
279. Arpeggios 366 39
280. Intervals 367 39
281. Intervals 368 39
282. Balance and Intonation: Diatonic Harmony 370 39
283. Balance and Intonation: Family Balance. 371 39
284. Balance and Intonation: Layered Tuning. 372 39
285. Balance and Intonation: Moving Chord Tones. 373 39
286. Expanding Intervals: Downward in Triads. 374 39
287. Expanding Intervals: Upward in Triads. 376 39
288. Rhythm. 377 40
289. Rhythm. 379 40
290. Rhythm. 380 40
291. Rhythmic Subdivision. 381 40
292. Rhythmic Subdivision. 383 40
293. Articulation and Dynamics 385 40
294. Etude 386 40
295. Chorale by Randall D. Standridge 388 41
296. Chorale by Roland Barrett. 389 41
297A. & 297B. Scale Chorale by Chris M. Bernotas. 391 41
298. Chorale by Robert Sheldon. 392 41
299. Chorale by Ralph Ford 395 41

Concert D♭ Major

300. Breathing and Long Tones. 397 42
301. Major Scale. 398 42
302. Scale Pattern 399 42
303. Scale Pattern 400 42
304. Scale Pattern 402 42
305. Flexibility 404 42
306. Arpeggios 405 42
307. Intervals 406 42
308. Balance and Intonation: Family Balance 407 43
309. Balance and Intonation: Layered Tuning 408 43
310. Expanding Intervals: Downward and Upward
     in Parallel Octaves 409 43
311. Articulation and Dynamics 410 43
312. Etude 411 43
313. Etude 412 43
314. Chorale by Andrew Boysen, Jr. 413 43
315. Chorale by Todd Stalter. 415 43

Concert B♭ Minor

316. Breathing and Long Tones. 417 44
317. Natural Minor Scale. 418 44
318. Harmonic and Melodic Minor Scales 419 44
319. Scale Pattern. 420 44
320. Scale Pattern. 422 44
321. Flexibility 423 44
322. Arpeggios 424 44

323. Intervals 425 44
324. Balance and Intonation: Layered Tuning. 426 44
325. Balance and Intonation: Moving Chord Tones 427 45
326. Expanding Intervals: Downward in Triads. 428 45
327. Articulation and Dynamics 429 45
328. Etude 430 45
329. Etude 432 45
330. Chorale by Michael Story. 433 45
331. Chorale by Robert Sheldon 434 45

Concert C Major

332. Breathing and Long Tones. 437 46
333. Major Scale. 438 46
334. Scale Pattern 439 46
335. Scale Pattern. 440 46
336. Flexibility 441 46
337. Arpeggios. 442 46
338. Intervals 443 46
339. Intervals 444 46
340. Balance and Intonation: Family Balance 445 46
341. Balance and Intonation: Layered Tuning. 446 47
342. Expanding Intervals: Downward in Parallel Fifths 447 47
343. Articulation and Dynamics 448 47
344. Etude 449 47
345. Etude 451 47
346. Chorale by Ralph Ford 453 47
347. Chorale: Largo from "New World Symphony"
     arranged by Michael Story 455 47

Concert A Minor

348. Breathing and Long Tones. 457 48
349. Natural Minor Scale 458 48
350. Harmonic and Melodic Minor Scales 459 48
351. Scale Pattern. 460 48
352. Flexibility 462 48
353. Arpeggios 463 48
354. Intervals 464 48
355. Intervals 465 48
356. Balance and Intonation: Diatonic Harmony 466 48
357. Balance and Intonation: Family Balance. 467 49
358. Expanding Intervals: Downward in Triads. 468 49
359. Articulation and Dynamics 469 49
360. Etude 470 49
361. Etude 472 49
362. Chorale by Todd Stalter 473 49
363. Chorale by Roland Barrett. 475 49

Concert G Major

364. Major Scale. 477 50
365. Balance and Intonation: Family Balance. 478 50
366. Etude 479 50
367. Chorale by Michael Story 480 50

Concert E Minor

368. Natural Minor Scale 481 50
369. Harmonic and Melodic Minor Scales 482 50
370. Balance and Intonation: Layered Tuning. 483 50
371. Etude 484 50
372. Chorale by Chris M. Bernotas 485 50

Advancing Rhythm and Meter

373. 6/8 Meter 486 51
374. 6/8 Meter 487 51
375. 6/8 Meter 488 51
376. 6/8 Meter 489 51
377. 6/8 Meter 490 51
378. 6/8 Meter 491 51
379. 6/8 Meter 492 51
380. 6/8 Meter 493 51
381. 6/8 Meter 494 51
382. 6/8 Meter 495 51
383. 6/8 Meter 496 52
384. 6/8 Meter 497 52
385. 6/8 Meter 498 52
386. 6/8 Meter 499 52
387. 6/8 Meter 500 52
388. 6/8 Meter 501 52
389. 6/8 Meter 502 52
390. 6/8 Meter 503 52
391. Changing Meters: 4/4 and 6/8 . . . . 504 52
392. Changing Meters: 3/4 and 6/8 . . . . 505 52
393. Triplets 506 53
394. Triplets 507 53
395. Triplets 508 53
396. Triplets 509 53
397. Triplets 510 53
398. Triplets 511 53
399. Triplets 512 53
400. Triplets 513 53
401. Triplets 514 53
402. Triplets 515 53
403. 3/8 Meter 516 54
404. 3/8 Meter 517 54
405. 9/8 Meter 518 54
406. 9/8 Meter 519 54
407. 12/8 Meter 520 54
408. 12/8 Meter 521 54
409. 5/8 Meter 522 54
410. 5/8 Meter 523 54
411. 7/8 Meter 524 54
412. 7/8 Meter 525 54

Expanded Fingering Chart 526 55
Percussion Appendix. 558 55
Percussive Arts Society International Drum Rudiments 560 55

Concert B♭ Major

1

PASSING THE TONIC

SOUND ADVICE

Remind students that good tone quality requires excellent posture, hand position, embouchure and breathing.

Encourage students to stagger breathe as necessary.

▶ Electric Bass/Synthesizer Bass: When being played

on a synthesizer bass, you may choose to have the part performed one octave lower than written. This part is transposed from the tuba part and does not appear in the score.

▶ Mallets: Feel free to add rolls for longer durations throughout the exercises in the book.

2 PASSING THE TONIC

SOUND ADVICE

Remind students that it is especially important to feel a steady inner pulse when playing whole notes.

▶ Percussion: Remind students to blend with the ensemble by make their rolls as smooth as possible.

3 # PASSING THE TONIC

SOUND ADVICE

Remind students to focus on their hand positions and embouchures while maintaining a steady stream of air.

Discuss with students the importance of holding notes for their full value.

Encourage students to sustain whole notes into the rest where appropriate.

▶ Percussion: Encourage students to use closed rolls, which release gently upon reaching the quarter note.

4 PASSING THE TONIC

SOUND ADVICE

Remind students to pay as much attention to the releases of their notes as they do to their attacks.

Have students practice playing releases that are beautiful and controlled.

▶ Percussion: Remind snare drum players to incorporate paradiddles, alternating between left- and right-hand lead.

5 **PASSING THE TONIC**

SOUND ADVICE

Be insistent about students keeping their feet flat on the floor with their backs away from the chair.

Have half of the students sing or hum this exercise, while the other half plays.

6 **BREATHING AND LONG TONES**

SOUND ADVICE

Use this exercise and others like it to foster full breaths using a variety of approaches and techniques, such as metered breathing, or quick, intense breaths.

Encourage students to exhale before inhaling to promote deep breathing.

▶ Percussion: Encourage students to use even and balanced hands when rolling.

7 ## BREATHING AND LONG TONES

SOUND ADVICE

This exercise and others like it provide an excellent opportunity to practice metered breathing. Encourage students to inhale gradually and continuously through every count of their rests.

▶ Percussion: Have students strive for even rolls without accents.

8 BREATHING AND LONG TONES

SOUND ADVICE

Have some brass students buzz this exercise on their mouthpiece, while other brass and/or woodwind players play it.

▶ Percussion: This exercise incorporates single strokes, paradiddles and double sticking for snare drum, and thumb rolls for tambourine.

9 **BREATHING AND LONG TONES**

SOUND ADVICE

Remind students to subdivide their counting throughout this exercise to ensure a steady tempo and accuracy of durations.

10   CONCERT B♭ MAJOR SCALE

SOUND ADVICE

Have students perform this exercise using a variety of articulations and dynamics.

▶ Percussion: This exercise incorporates the 9-stroke roll. Students might need to be reminded to keep the subdivision even throughout each roll.

11 SCALE PATTERN

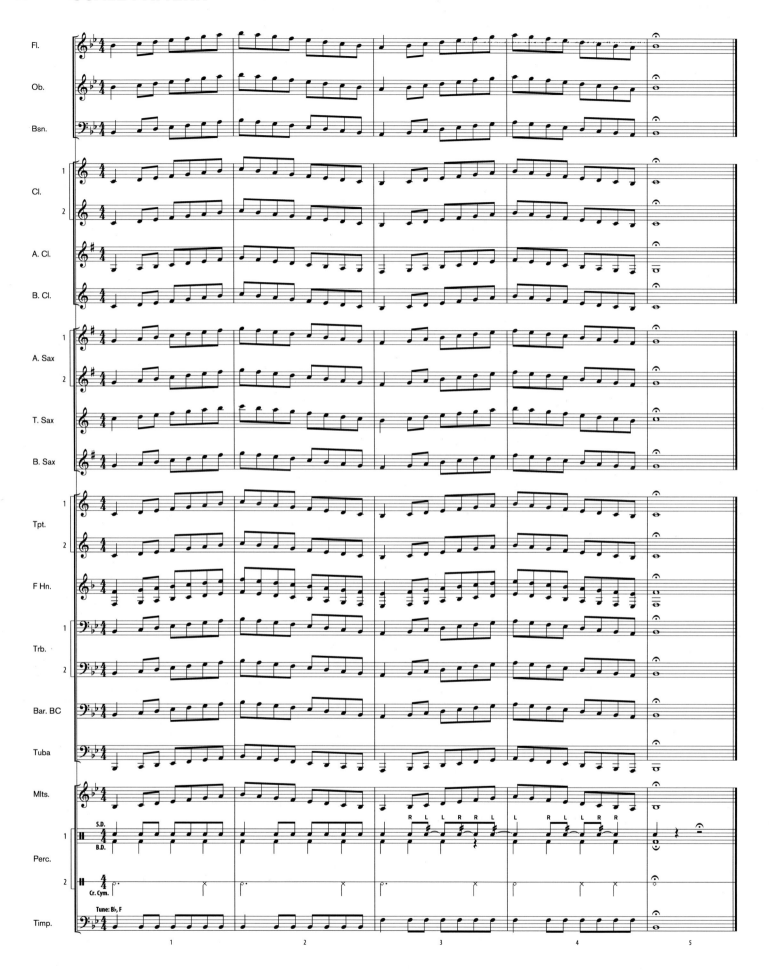

SOUND ADVICE

Work to maintain a consistent tone quality while moving throughout the range of the instrument.

▶ Percussion: This exercise incorporates alternating 5-stroke rolls.

12 **SCALE PATTERN**

SOUND ADVICE

Remind students to maintain a consistent volume as they ascend and descend throughout registers.

▶ Percussion: This exercise incorporates the flam, flam tap, drag and single paradiddle.

13 SCALE PATTERN

SOUND ADVICE

Have students evaluate the quality of their tone as they perform this exercise.

▶ Percussion: This exercise incorporates flams and flam taps.

14 **SCALE PATTERN**

SOUND ADVICE

Remind students not to clip short the last note of slurred passages.

▶ Snare Drum: Use repeated strokes for each hand to practice control and dexterity.

▶ Tambourine: Try to make both the shake and thumb roll clear and even in sound.

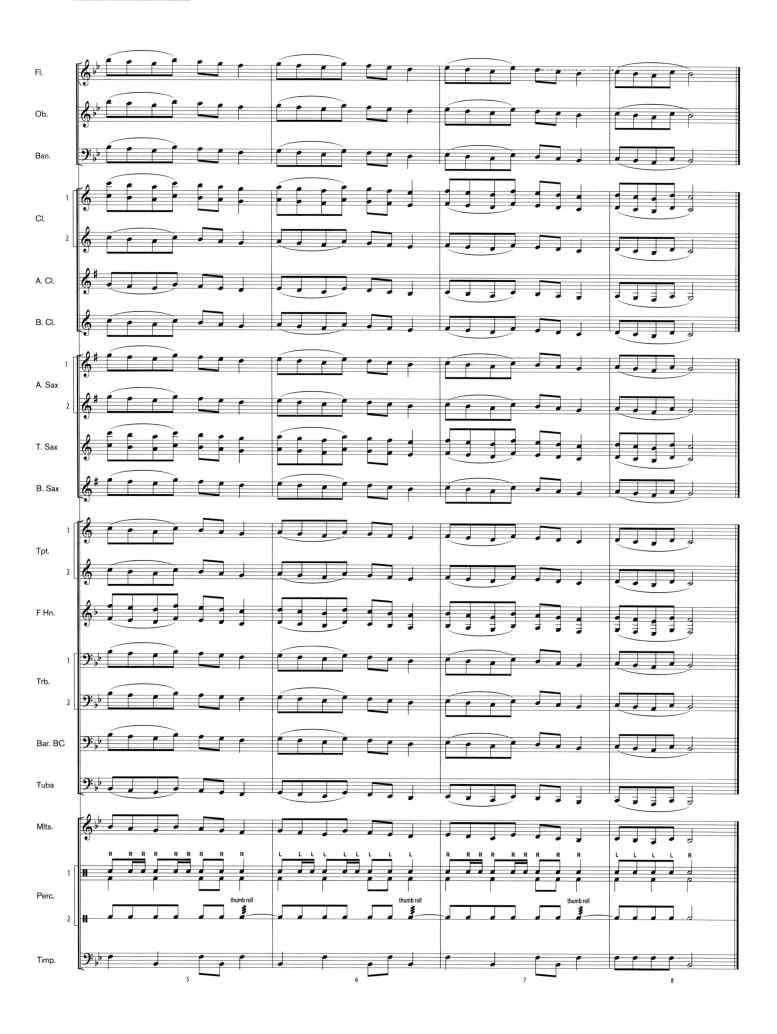

15   SCALE PATTERN

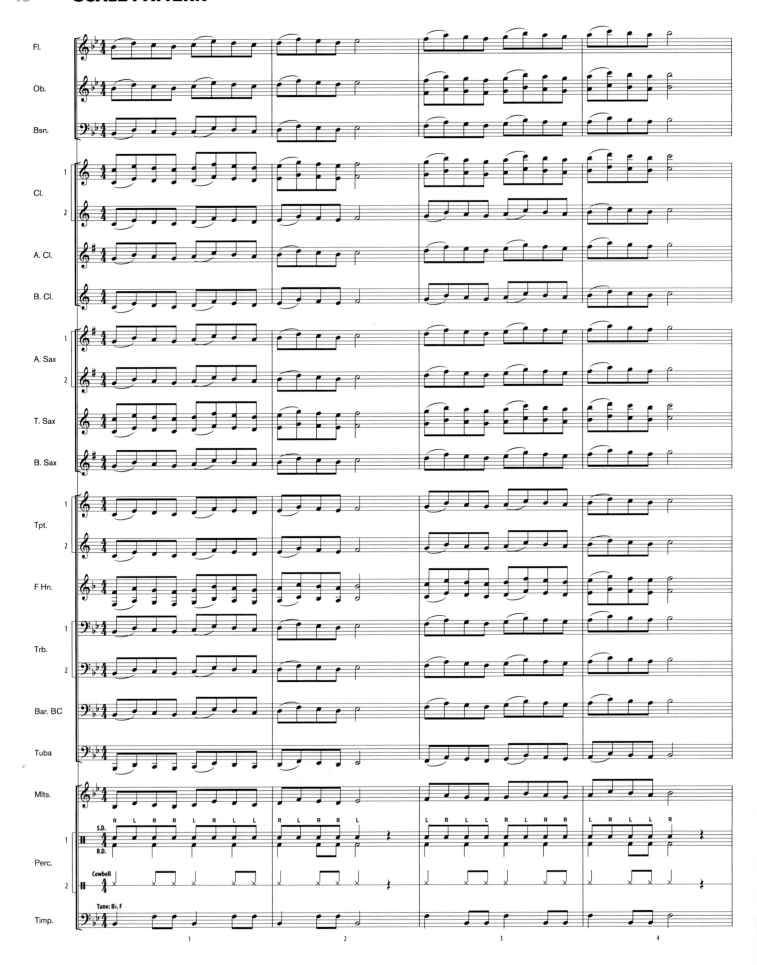

SOUND ADVICE

Have students practice this exercise with a variety of articulation patterns.

▶ Percussion: Create different sticking patterns for variety.

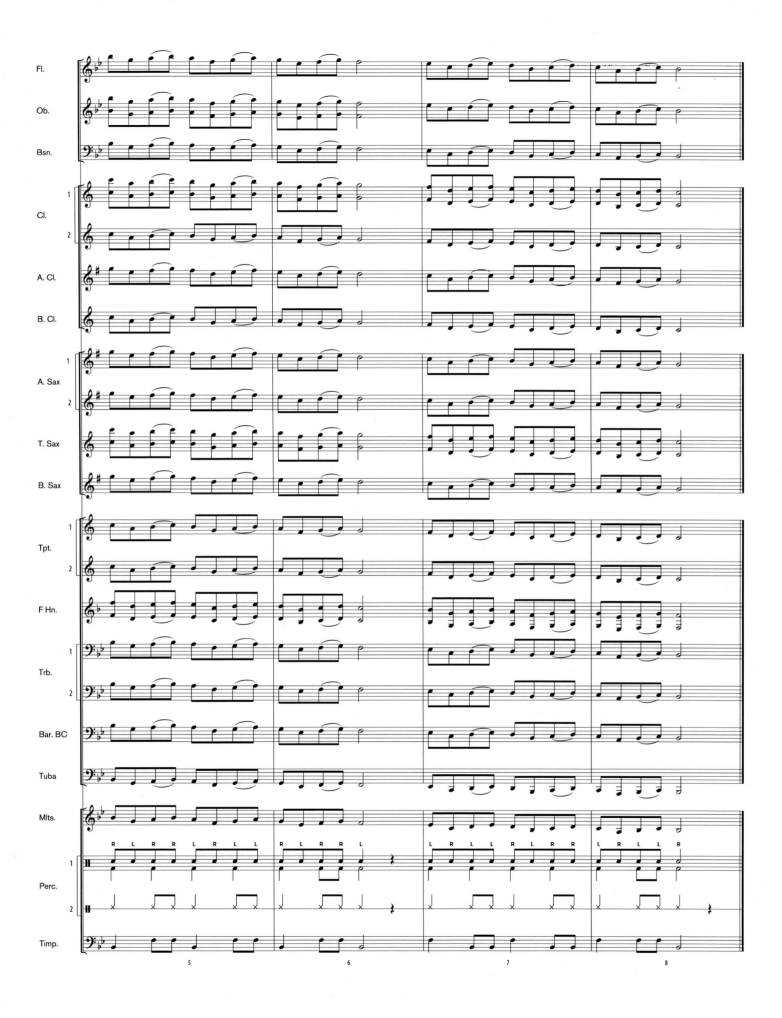

16 ## CHANGING SCALE RHYTHM

SOUND ADVICE

Remind students of the importance of a steady tempo and accurate internal subdivision of the pulse.

▶ Percussion: This exercise incorporates the 9-stroke and 17-stroke roll as well as a long roll. Depending on the tempo, students may want to use a triplet roll.

17 CONCERT B♭ CHROMATIC SCALE

SOUND ADVICE

Remind students to completely depress keys or valves, and move slides quickly before making a sound.

▶ Clarinets: Remind students to use the chromatic F♯ fingering for this exercise.

18 **FLEXIBILITY**

SOUND ADVICE

Remind students not to pinch their embouchures.

▶ Brass: Remind students to play higher notes by keeping a firm embouchure as they increase the speed of the airstream.

▶ Percussion: This exercise incorporates longer rolls. Students may need to be reminded to keep the subdivision even throughout each roll. These rolls can be open or closed.

19 **FLEXIBILITY**

SOUND ADVICE

▶ Brass: Remind players to keep their embouchures firm, but relaxed, when playing large downward leaps.

▶ Percussion: Remind students that long durations or fermatas without a roll should only be struck once. Also, remind students to dampen their instruments on rests.

20   ARPEGGIOS

SOUND ADVICE

▶ Percussion: This exercise incorporates the flam tap and flamacue.

21 ARPEGGIOS

SOUND ADVICE

Stress the importance of counting with subdivisions by having half of the students play this exercise, while the other half count aloud.

▶ Percussion: This exercise incorporates the flam paradiddle and flamacue.

22 **INTERVALS**

SOUND ADVICE

This exercise could also be performed with any number of students sustaining the first note as a drone to further develop intonation skills.

23 **INTERVALS**

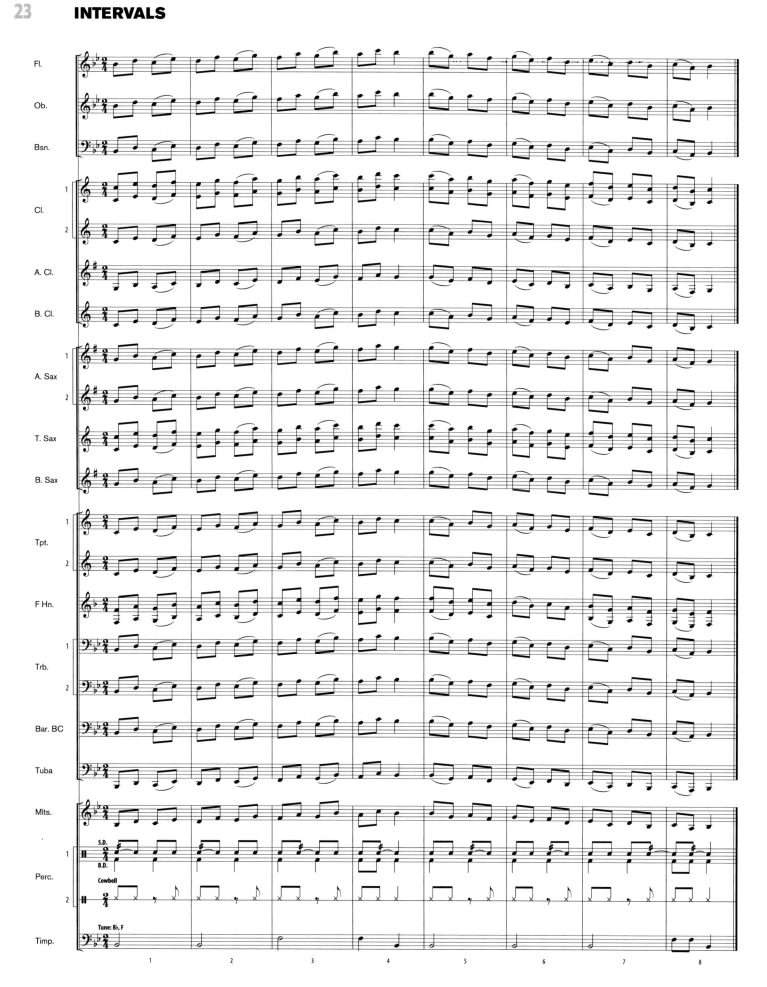

SOUND ADVICE

▶ Percussion: Students will practice 5-stroke rolls starting on downbeats and upbeats.

24

BALANCE AND INTONATION: PERFECT INTERVALS

SOUND ADVICE

Have some brass students buzz this exercise on their mouthpiece, while other brass and/or woodwind students play it.

25 **BALANCE AND INTONATION: DIATONIC HARMONY**

SOUND ADVICE

Have half of the students sing or hum this exercise, while the other half plays.

26 **BALANCE AND INTONATION: FAMILY BALANCE**

SOUND ADVICE

Have students discuss the concept of family balance and offer suggestions to improve their performance.

BALANCE AND INTONATION: LAYERED TUNING

SOUND ADVICE

In this exercise and others like it, intervals and triads are built by gradually adding one member of an interval or triad at a time, allowing students to focus on tuning vertical sonorities in a variety of contexts.

Encourage students to stagger breathe as necessary.

▶ Snare Drum: When the music indicates to turn the snares off, they stay off until they are marked to turn them back on.

28 BALANCE AND INTONATION: MOVING CHORD TONES

SOUND ADVICE

In this exercise and others like it, begin with each part playing one of the three notes of a triad. In subsequent measures, have each part cycle through the other two members of that triad, before arriving back to the original pitch. The goal is for each presentation of the triad to be performed equally well in tune as students practice playing the various members of a triad.

▶ Percussion: Remind students to work toward even triplets. This exercise incorporates the flam accent.

29 **BALANCE AND INTONATION: SHIFTING CHORD QUALITIES**

SOUND ADVICE

This exercise and others like it begin with the ensemble playing a major triad. In measure 2, the third of the triad moves downward a half-step to create a minor triad. In measure 3, the fifth of the triad moves downward a half step to create a diminished triad. Finally, measure 4 has the root of the triad move downward a half step to create a major triad. Cycling through these chord qualities will help foster horizontal and vertical tuning, as well as balance, blend and internalizing pitch.

Enharmonic note names are used to allow directors the opportunity to discuss why composers would use certain spellings that would be most appropriate for certain chords.

▶ Snare Drum: This exercise provides an opportunity to work on open and closed rolls.

▶ Timpani: Use your ear to tune the drum down in half steps.

30 EXPANDING INTERVALS: DOWNWARD IN PARALLEL OCTAVES

SOUND ADVICE

From their starting pitch in this exercise and other exercises like it, students move to a pitch one half step away before returning back to the original pitch. Following that pattern, they gradually increase the distance of that interval by a half step each time.

▶ Clarinets: Students may wish to keep their right hand down when moving to the lower notes.

31   ## EXPANDING INTERVALS: DOWNWARD IN PARALLEL FIFTHS

SOUND ADVICE

This exercise offers a wonderful opportunity to develop the skills of tuning horizontally, as well as vertically, while attending to balance, blend and intonation.

The starting unison B♭ of this exercise can help students establish pitch before beginning the interval study.

32 EXPANDING INTERVALS: DOWNWARD IN TRIADS

SOUND ADVICE
This exercise offers teachers an excellent opportunity to discuss the tuning of triads.

33 EXPANDING INTERVALS: UPWARD IN PARALLEL OCTAVES

SOUND ADVICE

Remind students to keep their shoulders relaxed, especially when moving upward in this exercise.

34 EXPANDING INTERVALS: UPWARD IN TRIADS

SOUND ADVICE

Help students achieve a blended and balanced ensemble sound in this exercise.

35   ## RHYTHM

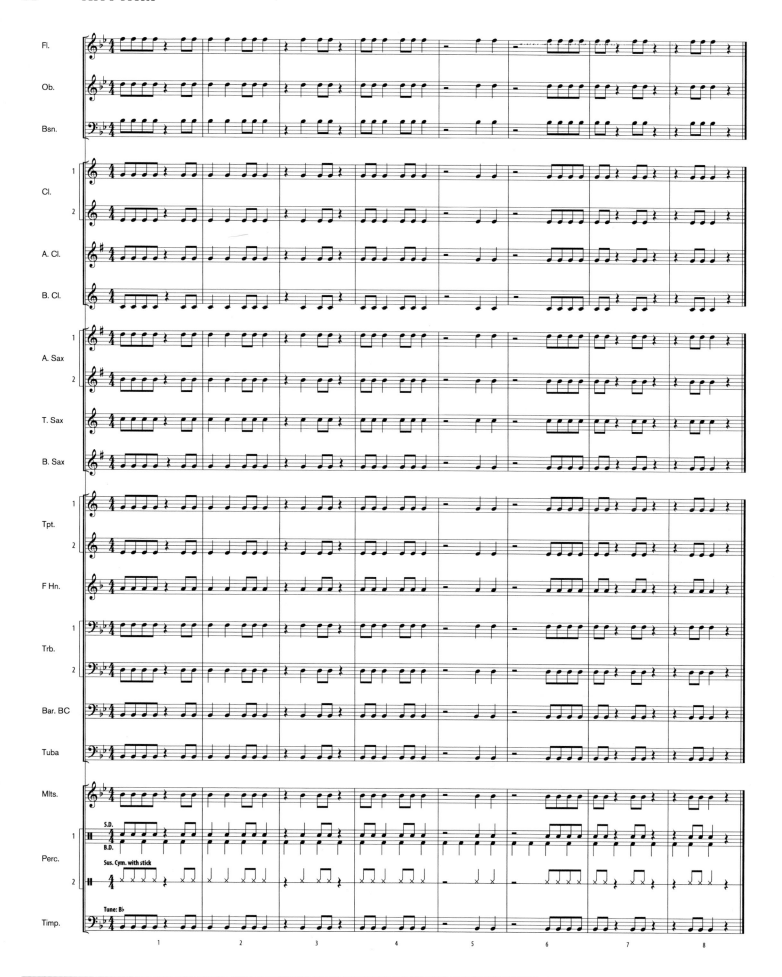

SOUND ADVICE

Have half the ensemble clap the rhythm of this exercise, while the other half plays, then vice versa.

▶ Percussion: Remind percussion to dampen their instruments on rests.

36   RHYTHM

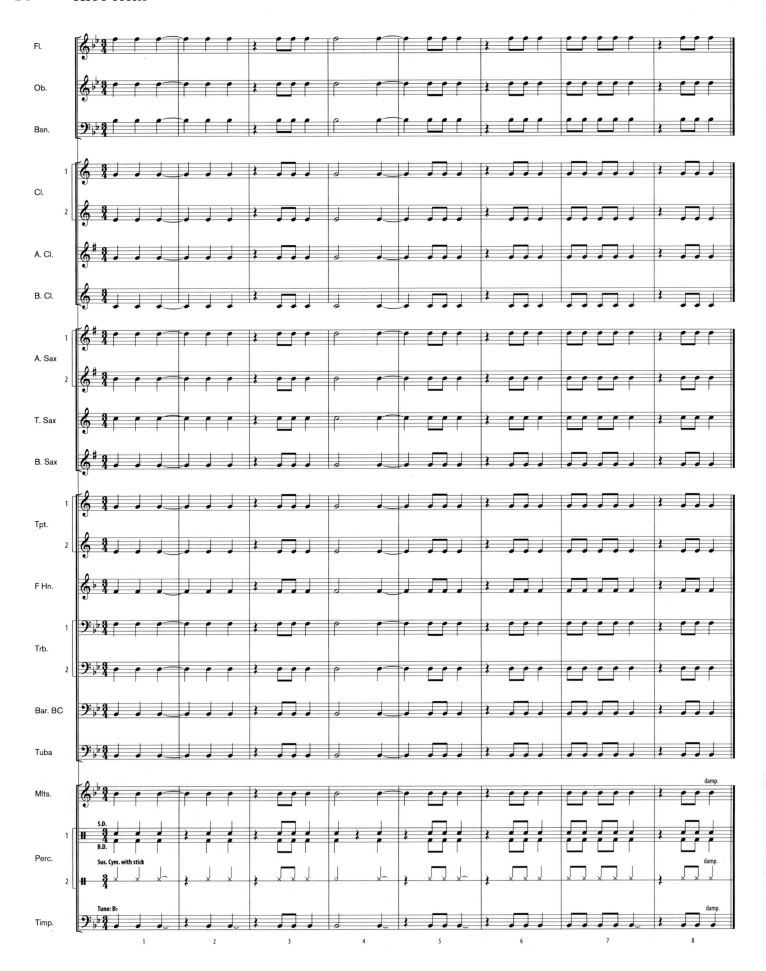

SOUND ADVICE

▶ Mallets: Use finger dampening for the last note.

37   **RHYTHM**

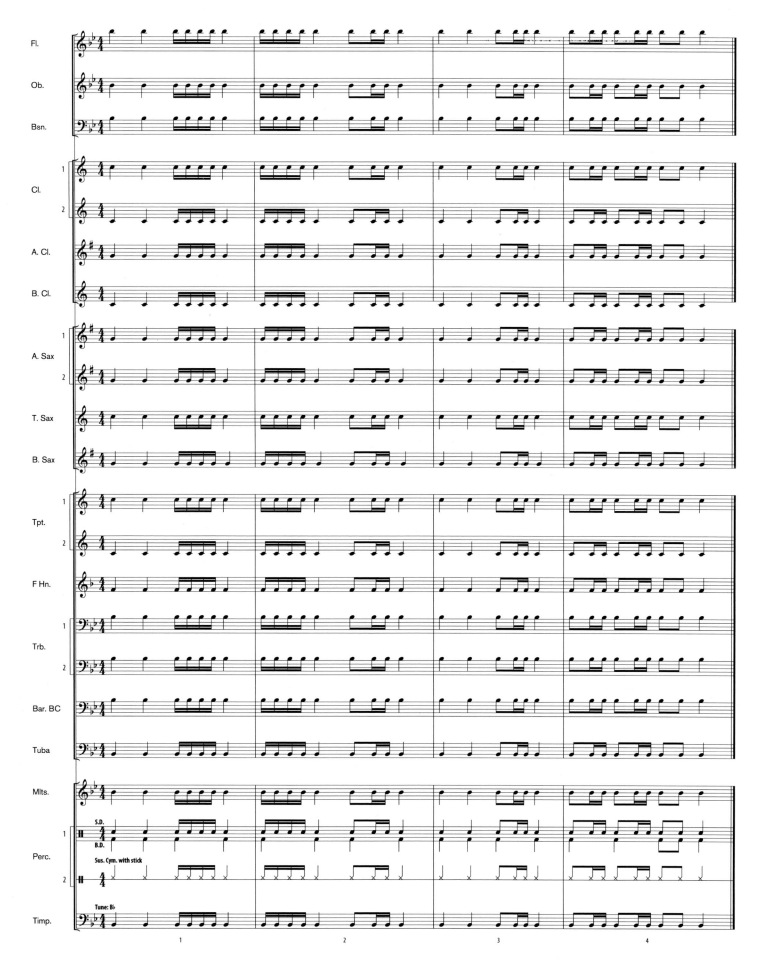

SOUND ADVICE

Have students write in the counting and subdivision and then clap the exercise before actually playing it.

38 RHYTHM

SOUND ADVICE

This exercise can be played in 6 or in 2. With either choice students should count all six beats to ensure accuracy.

39   RHYTHM

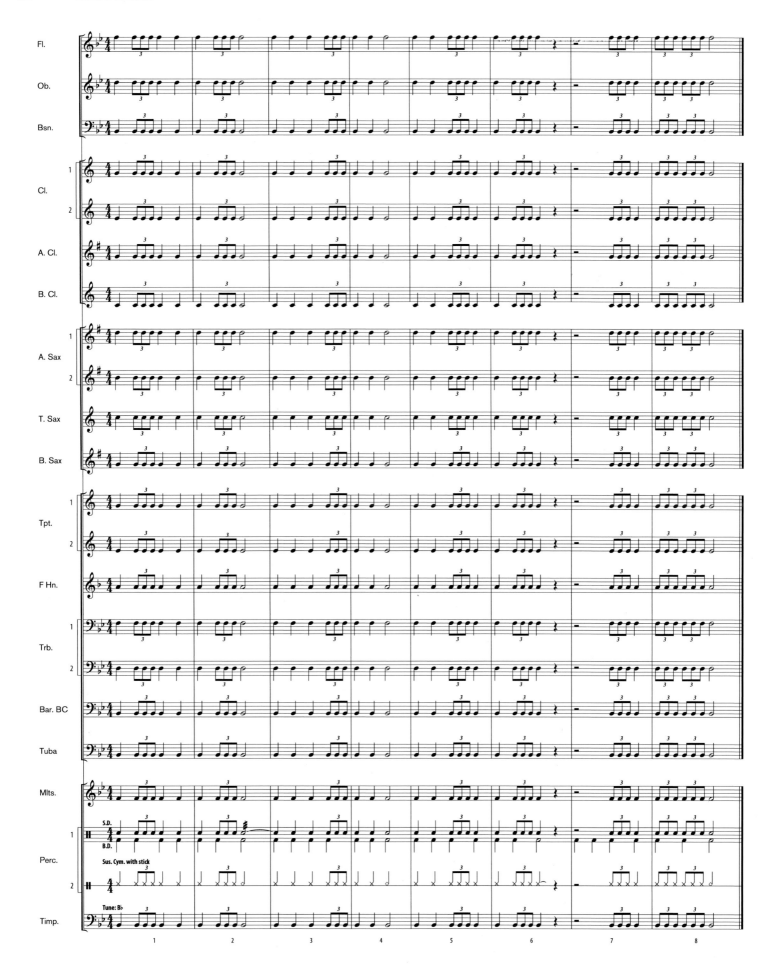

SOUND ADVICE

Have students work toward keeping the three notes of the triplet even in duration.

40   **RHYTHMIC SUBDIVISION**

SOUND ADVICE
Use this exercise to ensure the rhythmic subdivision of longer durations.

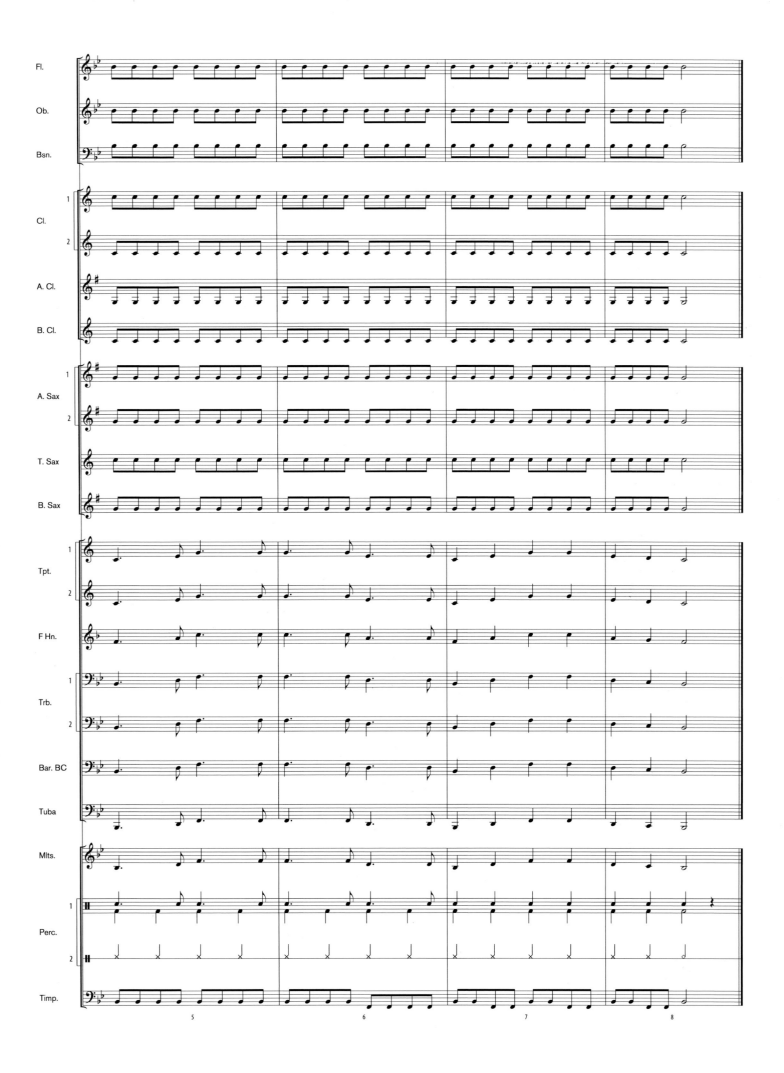

41   RHYTHMIC SUBDIVISION

SOUND ADVICE

Attending to the rhythmic subdivision of this exercise will help students maintain a steady tempo with syncopated rhythms.

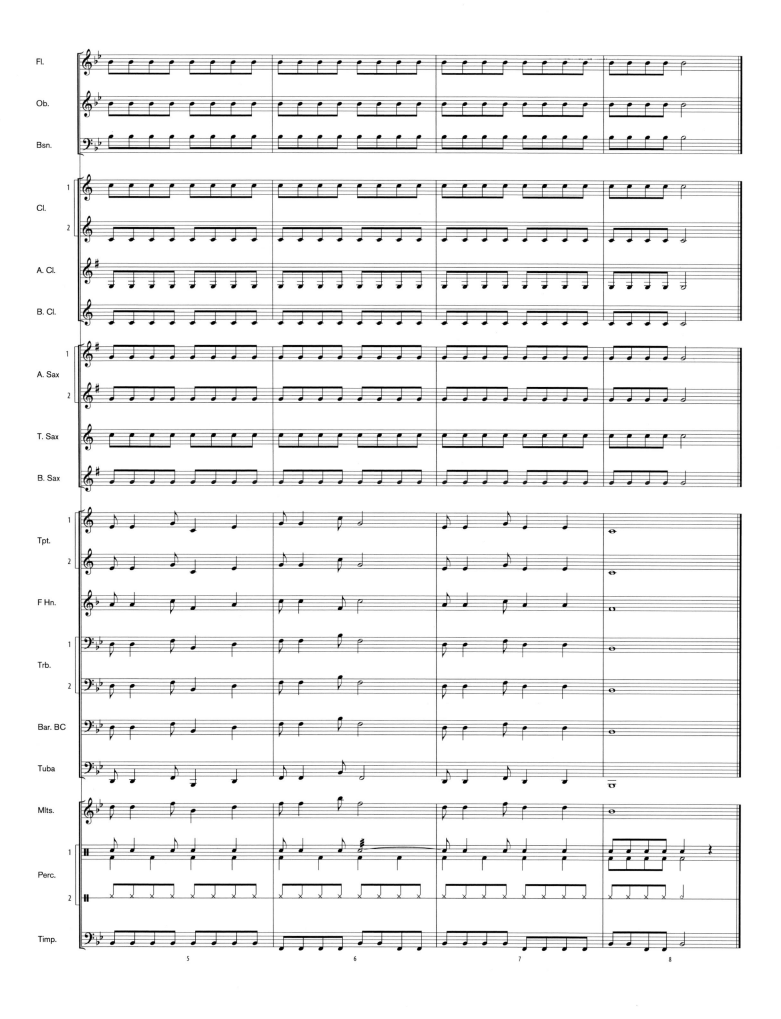

42 RHYTHMIC SUBDIVISION

SOUND ADVICE

Remind students to subdivide their counting throughout this exercise to ensure a steady tempo and accuracy of rhythm.

43   METER

SOUND ADVICE
Have students write in the counting and then clap the exercise before actually playing it.

44   **PHRASING**

SOUND ADVICE

Discuss with students appropriate places to breathe in this exercise.

45 PHRASING

SOUND ADVICE

Discuss with students how they can make the contrasts of these phrases more noticeable.

46   ARTICULATION

SOUND ADVICE

Remind students to work toward vivid contrasts of articulation in this exercise.

▶ Timpani: Make sure that students dampen for staccato pitches.

47 **DYNAMICS**

SOUND ADVICE

Encourage students to make their crescendos and decrescendos even and gradual.

Have the ensemble work toward making contrasts in dynamics more apparent.

▶ Percussion: Remind students to dampen on the rests.

48 **ETUDE**

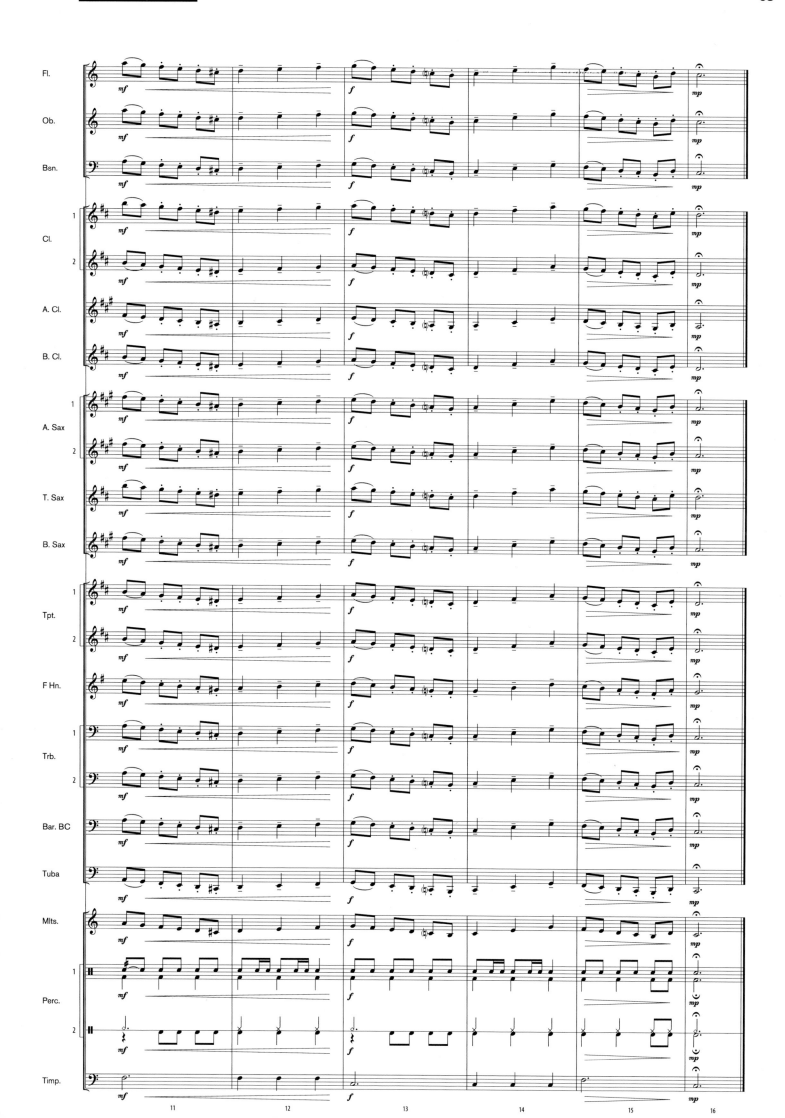

49 **ETUDE**

50

CHORALE: JESU, MEINE ZUVERSICHT

Johann Cruger (1598–1662)
Arranged by Todd Stalter

51 **CHORALE**

Michael Story (ASCAP)

52 **CONCERT B♭ MAJOR SCALE & CHORALE**

Chris M. Bernotas (ASCAP)

SOUND ADVICE

This chorale and others like it, is a harmonized scale. Each student's part has two lines: the scale (the top line, A), and their part in the chorale (the bottom line, B).73 Directors can choose a single student, a section, a family, or any other combination of instrumentalists to play the

scale while the rest of the ensemble plays the chorale setting.

▶ Percussion: Note that Percussion 1 and 2 do not have an A or B label. These parts may be used to accompany the scale or as part of the chorale.

53 **CHORALE**

Chris M. Bernotas (ASCAP)

54 **CHORALE**

Randall D. Standridge (ASCAP)

55 **CHORALE**

Andrew Boysen, Jr.

56 ## CHORALE

Ralph Ford (ASCAP)

57 **CHORALE**

Robert Sheldon

58 **CHORALE**

Roland Barrett

59   # CHORALE

Chris M. Bernotas (ASCAP)

60 CHORALE

Rossano Galante

Concert G Minor

61 **PASSING THE TONIC**

SOUND ADVICE

For some of the minor key exercises, triads are used so the minor tonality is heard.

Remind students that it is especially important to keep a steady pulse when playing whole notes.

62 BREATHING AND LONG TONES

SOUND ADVICE

Remind students to focus on their hand positions and embouchures, while maintaining a steady stream of air.

63   ## CONCERT G NATURAL MINOR SCALE

SOUND ADVICE

Remind students to depress valves or keys firmly and completely.

▶ Snare Drum: Have students work toward even 9-stroke rolls.

64
CONCERT G HARMONIC AND MELODIC MINOR SCALES

SOUND ADVICE
▶ Snare Drum: For variety, have students reverse the sticking on this exercise.

65 SCALE PATTERN

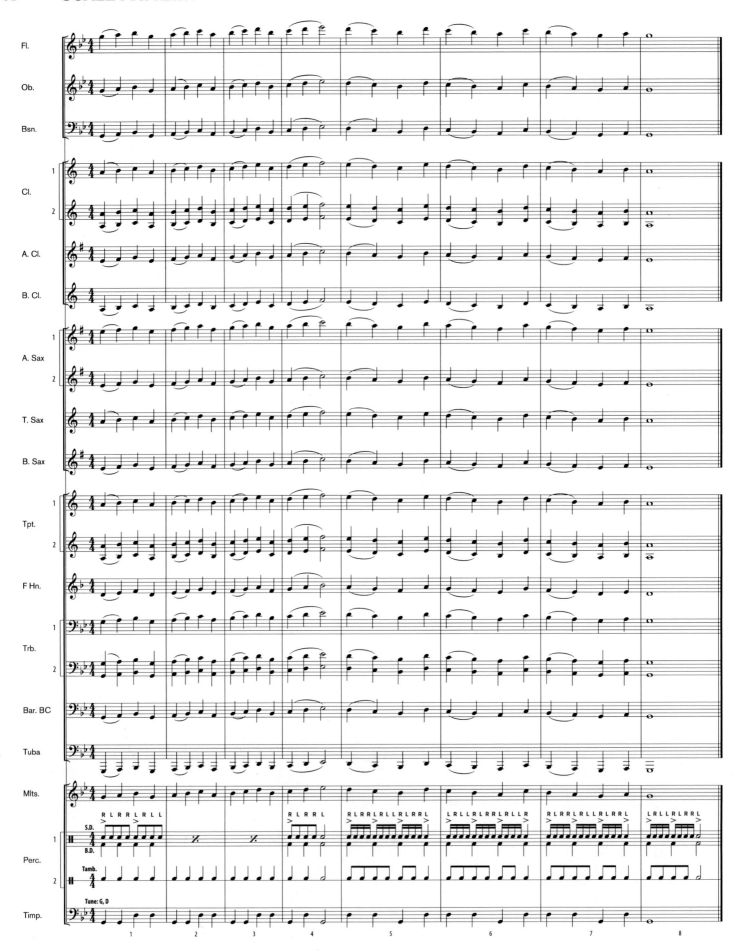

SOUND ADVICE
Remind students not to clip the last note of a slur.

66 **CONCERT G CHROMATIC SCALE**

SOUND ADVICE

▶ Clarinet: Remind students to use the chromatic F♯ fingering.

▶ Snare Drum: This exercise incorporates the lesson 25 rudiment.

67   **FLEXIBILITY**

SOUND ADVICE

For some of the minor key exercises, triads are used so the minor tonality is heard.

▶ Horn: Encourage students playing on double horns to use the B♭ fingerings (with trigger) for this exercise.

▶ Snare Drum: This exercise incorporates the drag rudiment.

68   **FLEXIBILITY**

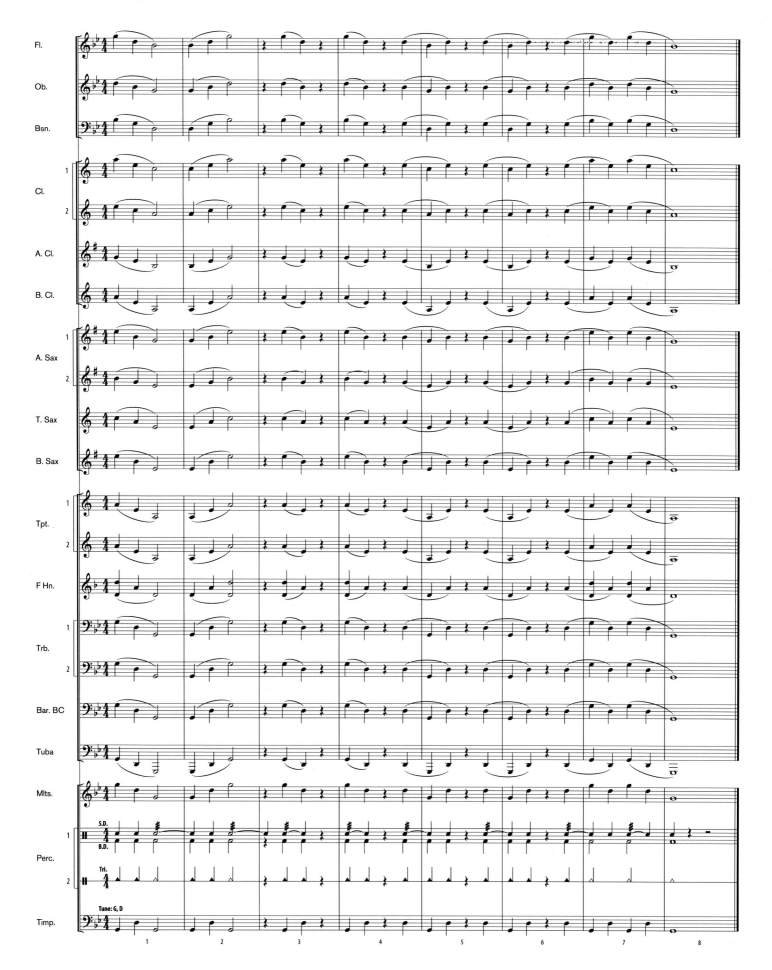

SOUND ADVICE
▶ Percussion: Remind percussion to dampen their instruments on rests.

69 **ARPEGGIOS**

SOUND ADVICE

Help students find the correct height and placement of their music stand to ensure good posture and playing position, as well as their ability to watch the teacher.

▶ Horn: This exercise can be played entirely on the B♭ side of the horn to increase flexibility: T12.

▶ Snare Drum: This exercise incorporates the single drag tap

70 **ARPEGGIOS**

SOUND ADVICE
Discuss with students appropriate places for breath marks in this exercise.

71   INTERVALS

SOUND ADVICE

Be insistent about students keeping their feet flat on the floor with their backs away from the chair.

72 **INTERVALS**

SOUND ADVICE

Discuss with students which form of minor scale this exercise is based upon.

73 BALANCE AND INTONATION: DIATONIC HARMONY

SOUND ADVICE

Help students achieve a blended and balanced sound in this exercise.

74 **BALANCE AND INTONATION: MOVING CHORD TONES**

SOUND ADVICE

Ask students to work for clearly defined movement between pitches.

75 BALANCE AND INTONATION: LAYERED TUNING

SOUND ADVICE

Have students hum exercises until they are comfortable with the idea of singing them.

76 **BALANCE AND INTONATION: FAMILY BALANCE**

SOUND ADVICE

Discuss with members of the ensemble the qualities of family balance.

77 **EXPANDING INTERVALS: DOWNWARD IN PARALLEL FIFTHS**

SOUND ADVICE

The starting unison G of this exercise can help students establish pitch before beginning the interval study.

78   **EXPANDING INTERVALS: UPWARD IN PARALLEL THIRDS**

SOUND ADVICE

Have students work toward consistent tone quality as they ascend in this exercise.

▶ Snare Drum: Remind student to disengage the snares for this exercise.

79 **RHYTHM**

SOUND ADVICE

Remind students to subdivide their counting throughout this exercise to ensure a steady tempo and accuracy of rhythm.

▶ Percussion: Remind students to dampen on rests.

80   **RHYTHM**

SOUND ADVICE
Have students write in the counting and subdivision before playing this exercise.

81 **RHYTHM**

SOUND ADVICE

Remind students not to clip quarter notes and dotted quarter notes in this exercise.

▶ Snare Drum: This exercise incorporates the drag paradiddle #1.

82 **RHYTHMIC SUBDIVISION**

SOUND ADVICE

Remind students not to change tempo when moving from less active rhythms to more active rhythms within a passage.

83 # RHYTHMIC SUBDIVISION

SOUND ADVICE

Have half the class conduct this exercise, while the other half performs it as written.

▶ Snare Drum: Encourage students to try alternating sticking (R/L), and for variety try playing with ALL right hand, then ALL left-hand strokes.

84 ARTICULATION AND DYNAMICS

SOUND ADVICE

Remind students to work toward a gradual crescendo and decrescendo as they exaggerate contrasts in articulation.

▶ Mallets: Use finger dampening for the staccato pitches.

▶ Timpani: Make sure students dampen for staccato pitches

85 **ETUDE**

86 **CHORALE**

Robert Sheldon

87 **CHORALE**

Michael Story (ASCAP)

88 **CONCERT G MINOR SCALE & CHORALE**

Chris M. Bernotas (ASCAP)

89 **CHORALE**

Andrew Boysen, Jr.

90

CHORALE

Rossano Galante

Sad and expressive, freely

Concert E♭ Major

91 **PASSING THE TONIC**

SOUND ADVICE

Remind students that good tone quality requires excellent posture, hand position, embouchure and breathing.

92   PASSING THE TONIC

SOUND ADVICE

Remind students to keep a steady stream of air as they pass the tonic through the ensemble.

93 PASSING THE TONIC

SOUND ADVICE

To encourage unified playing, discuss with students precisely how long and where they should breathe.

94 **PASSING THE TONIC**

SOUND ADVICE

Remind students not to change tempo when moving from less active rhythms to more active rhythms within a passage.

95 PASSING THE TONIC

SOUND ADVICE

Encourage students to stagger breathe as necessary.

96 BREATHING AND LONG TONES

SOUND ADVICE

Encourage students to breathe throughout each of the rests.

97   BREATHING AND LONG TONES

SOUND ADVICE

Encourage students to exhale before inhaling to promote deep breathing.

98 **BREATHING AND LONG TONES**

SOUND ADVICE

▶ Brass: Remind students to strive for a free and open tone when playing in higher registers.

▶ Snare Drum: This exercise offers students the opportunity to practice 5-stroke, 9-stroke and 17-stroke rolls.

99 BREATHING AND LONG TONES

SOUND ADVICE

This exercise offers a great opportunity for students to sing their pitches once they are comfortable humming.

100   **CONCERT E♭ MAJOR SCALE**

SOUND ADVICE

▶ Snare Drum: This exercise incorporates the 13-stroke roll.

101   SCALE PATTERN

SOUND ADVICE

▶ Snare Drum: Try playing paradiddles with these sixteenth notes. The half-note rolls are closed. You can experiment with both open and closed rolls depending on the style of music.

102 **SCALE PATTERN**

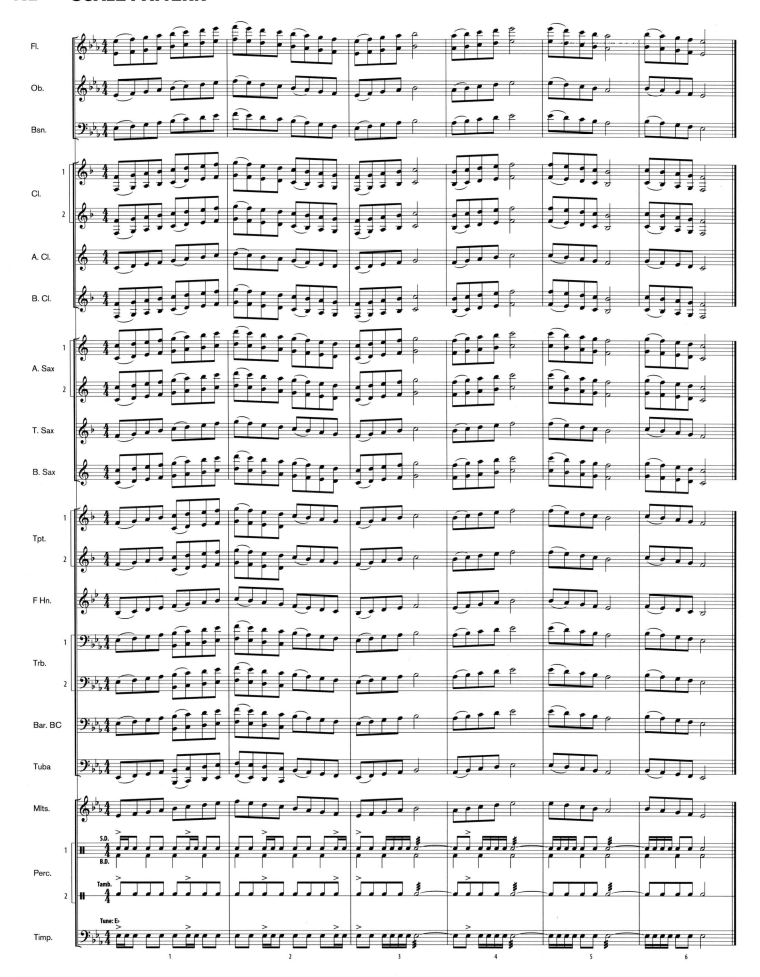

SOUND ADVICE
This exercise offers a great opportunity to substitute various articulation patterns.

103 SCALE PATTERN

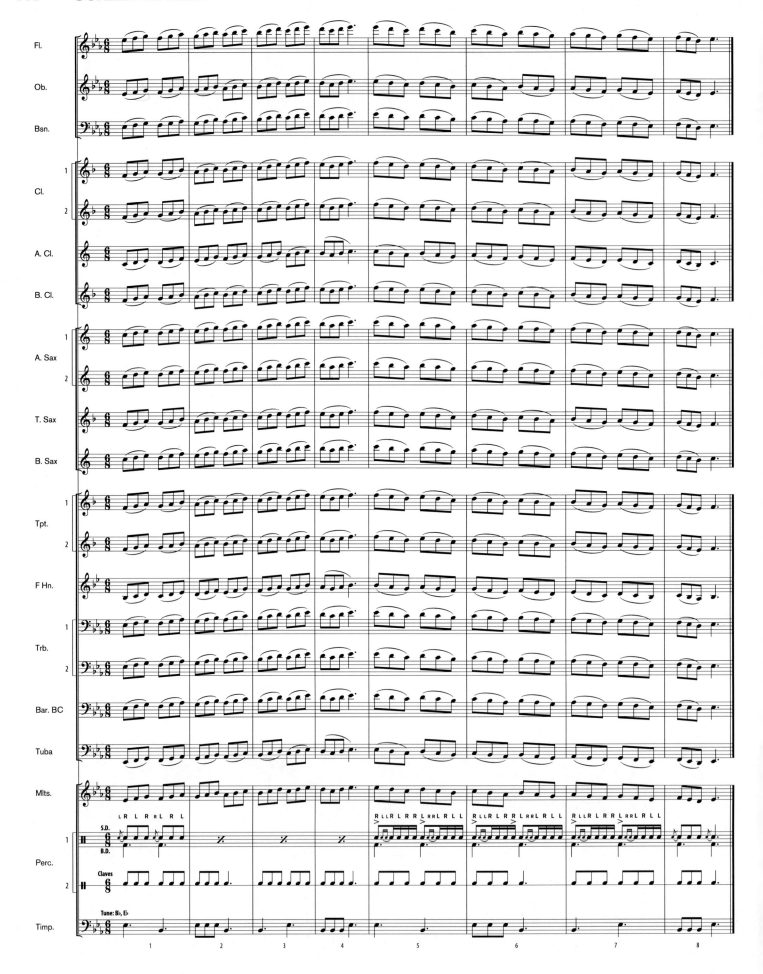

SOUND ADVICE

▶ Snare Drum: This exercise incorporates the flam accent and the drag paradiddle #1.

104 **SCALE PATTERN**

SOUND ADVICE
Remind students to completely depress keys or valves, and move slides quickly before making a sound.

105 **SCALE PATTERN**

SOUND ADVICE

▶ Snare Drum: Discuss with students the stickings for this exercise. Encourage them to create other appropriate sticking patterns.

106 **CHANGING SCALE RHYTHM**

SOUND ADVICE

To encourage unified playing, discuss with students precisely how long and when they should breathe.

107 **CONCERT E♭ CHROMATIC SCALE**

SOUND ADVICE

▶ Clarinet and Bass Clarinet: Remind students to use the chromatic B fingering in the lower octave and the chromatic F♯ fingering in the upper octave.

▶ Alto Clarinet: Remind students to use the chromatic F♯ fingering.

108 **FLEXIBILITY**

SOUND ADVICE

This exercise could also be played in common time.

▶ Horn: Encourage students to play this entire exercise on the F side with the 1st valve.

109   **FLEXIBILITY**

SOUND ADVICE

▶ Snare Drum: This exercise incorporates the 13-stroke roll and the 17-stroke roll.

▶ Horn: Encourage students to play this entire exercise on the F side with the 1st valve.

110 **ARPEGGIOS**

SOUND ADVICE

Experiment by having some of the ensemble sustain this major triad, while others play the exercise as written.

111   **ARPEGGIOS**

SOUND ADVICE
▶ Snare Drum: This exercise incorporates the flam paradiddle.

112 **INTERVALS**

SOUND ADVICE

This exercise can also be performed by having students slur between the two half notes of each measure.

113   INTERVALS

SOUND ADVICE

▶ Brass: Remind players to keep their embouchures firm, but relaxed, when playing large downward leaps.

▶ Snare Drum: This exercise provides a good opportunity for practicing the flam accent.

114 BALANCE AND INTONATION: PERFECT INTERVALS

SOUND ADVICE

Notice that the timpani sustains a roll through this entire exercise.

115   **BALANCE AND INTONATION: DIATONIC HARMONY**

SOUND ADVICE

Discuss with students the appropriate place to breathe in this exercise.

116 **BALANCE AND INTONATION: FAMILY BALANCE**

SOUND ADVICE

Have students discuss the concept of family balance and offer suggestions to improve their performance.

117 BALANCE AND INTONATION: LAYERED TUNING

SOUND ADVICE

Have students work toward melding their sound into that of the ensemble.

▶ Percussion: Discuss with percussionists the difference between a Mark Tree, Bell Tree and Wind Chimes.

118 BALANCE AND INTONATION: LAYERED TUNING

SOUND ADVICE

▶ Percussion: Practice controlling the dynamics and balance within the ensemble, especially when playing more active rhythms.

119 BALANCE AND INTONATION: SHIFTING CHORD QUALITIES

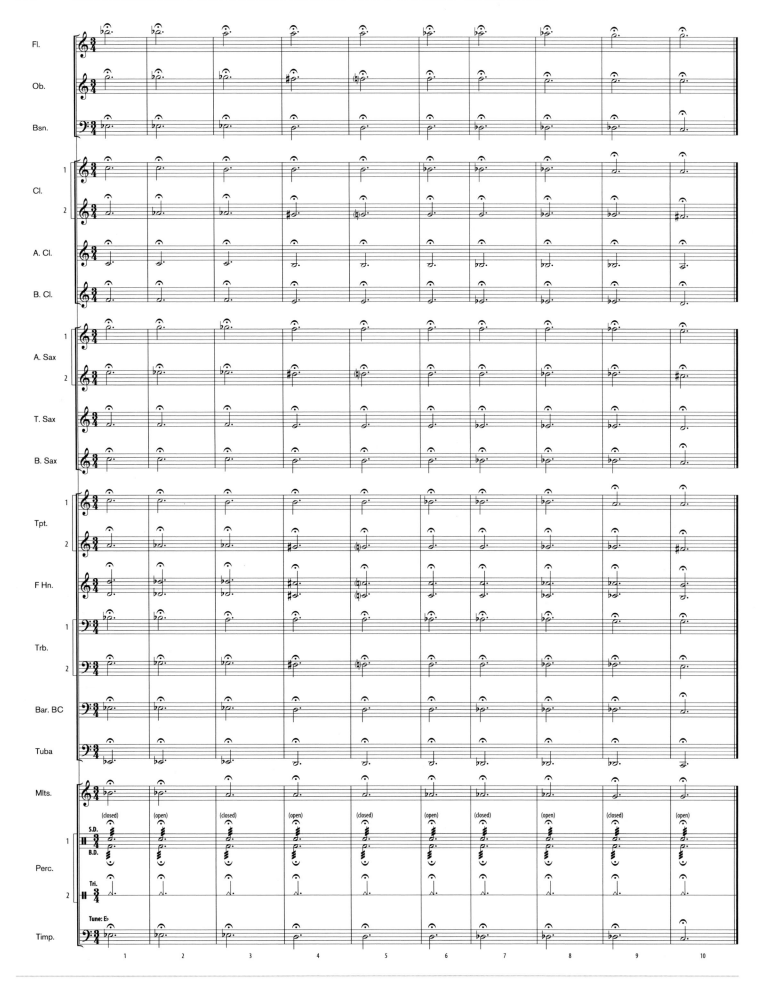

SOUND ADVICE

Have half of the ensemble hum or sing this exercise, while the other half plays it.

▶ Timpani: Use your ear to tune the drum down in half steps.

120 EXPANDING INTERVALS: DOWNWARD IN PARALLEL OCTAVES

SOUND ADVICE

▶ Percussion: Encourage students to work on developing equal strength in both hands.

▶ Snare Drum: Have students use double-stroke metered rolls to help them concentrate on subdividing.

121   **EXPANDING INTERVALS: DOWNWARD IN PARALLEL FIFTHS**

SOUND ADVICE

Have some brass students buzz this exercise on their mouthpiece, while other brass and/or woodwind students play it.

122 EXPANDING INTERVALS: DOWNWARD IN TRIADS

SOUND ADVICE

▶ Percussion: For instruments that ring, don't forget to dampen on the rest.

▶ Snare Drum: This might be a good time to practice accuracy with paradiddles.

123   **EXPANDING INTERVALS: UPWARD IN PARALLEL OCTAVES**

SOUND ADVICE

Remind students to pay as much attention to the releases of their notes as they do to their attacks.

▶ Clarinet and Bass Clarinet: Remind students to use the chromatic F♯ fingering for this exercise.

124 EXPANDING INTERVALS: UPWARD IN TRIADS

SOUND ADVICE

▶ Clarinet 1: Remind students to use the chromatic F♯ fingering for this exercise.

125   RHYTHM

SOUND ADVICE

Make certain students play full durations of each note, especially at slower tempos.

▶ Percussion: Remind students to dampen on the rests.

126   RHYTHM

SOUND ADVICE

Stress the importance of counting with subdivisions by having half of the students play this exercise, while the other half counts aloud.

127 RHYTHM

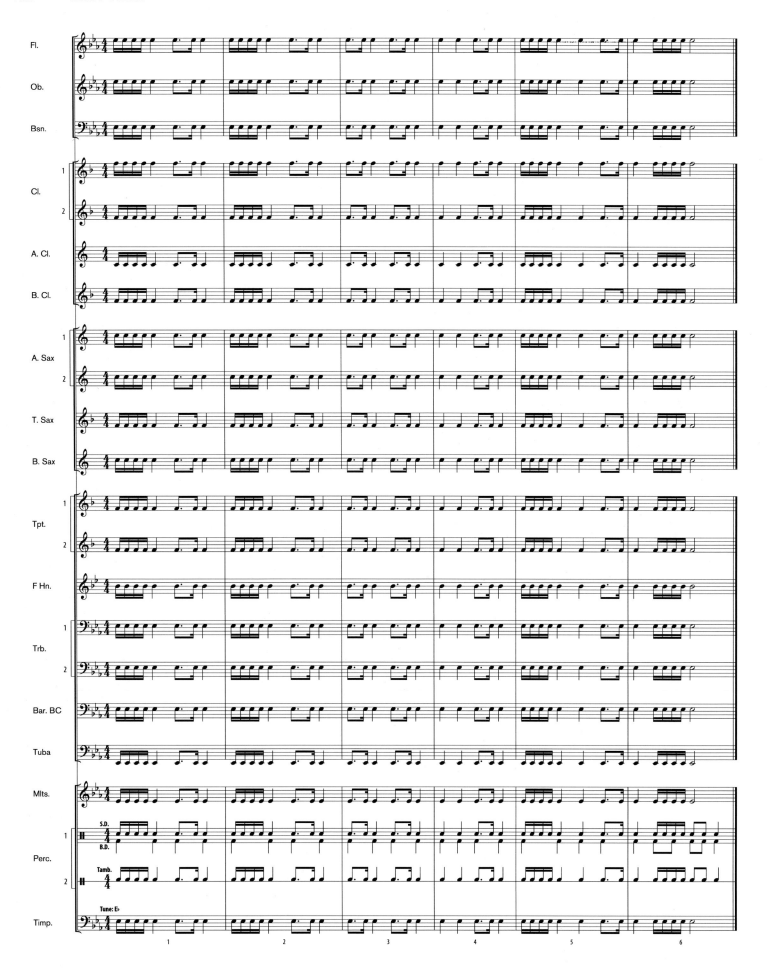

SOUND ADVICE

Remind students not to change tempo when moving from less active rhythms to more active rhythms within a passage.

128 RHYTHM

SOUND ADVICE
Remind students not to clip notes shorter than indicated.

129   **RHYTHM**

SOUND ADVICE

Have students practice counting the subdivision of measure 7 as it moves from triple to duple.

▶ Bass Drum: Make certain the solo in measure 3 is performed with confidence.

130   **RHYTHMIC SUBDIVISION**

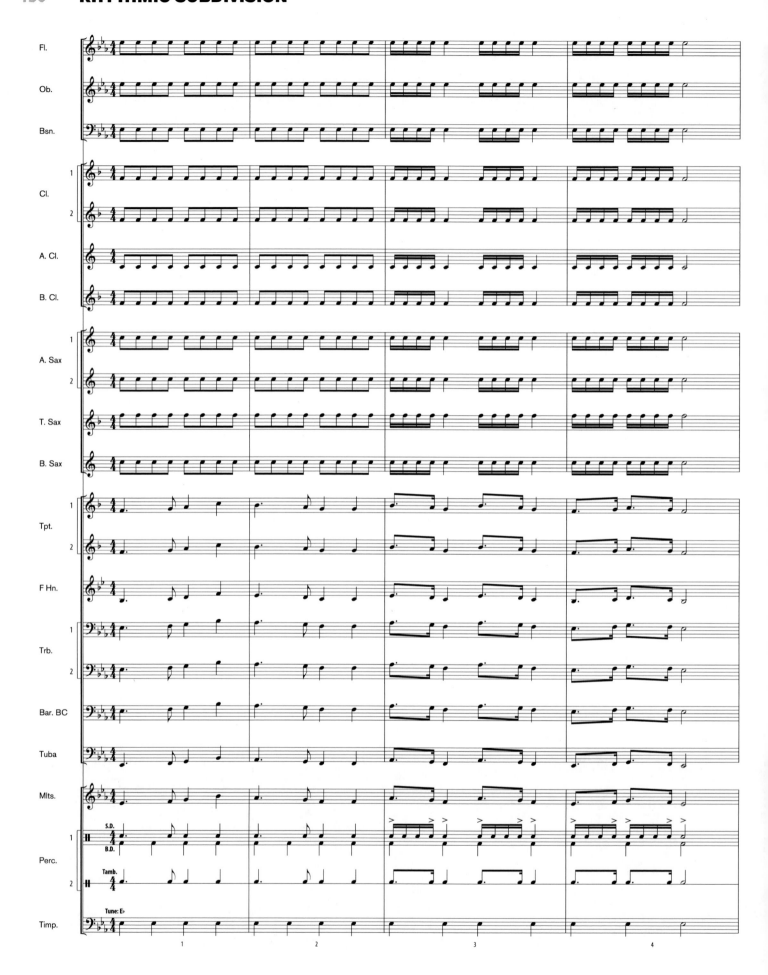

SOUND ADVICE

Remind students not to increase their volume as the rhythm becomes more active.

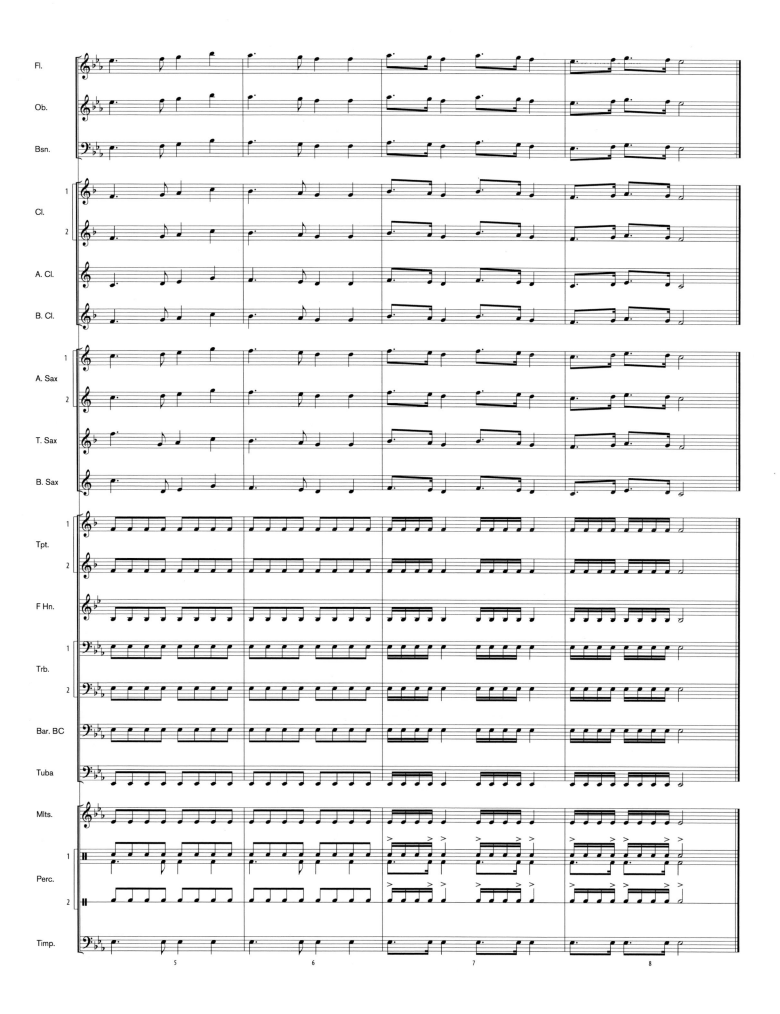

131 **RHYTHMIC SUBDIVISION**

SOUND ADVICE

Remind students that half of the ensemble is playing the subdivision, while the other half is playing the melodic passage.

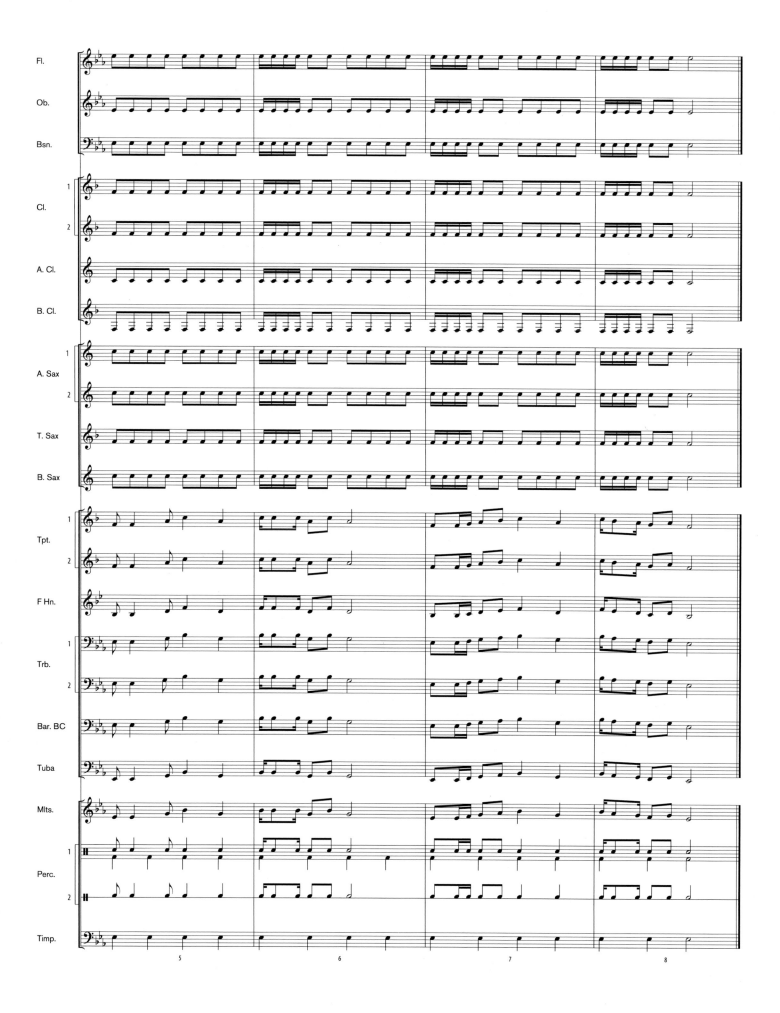

132 RHYTHMIC SUBDIVISION

SOUND ADVICE
Experiment with different articulations to provide variety for this exercise.

133   METER

SOUND ADVICE

Remind students to play each note for its full duration.

134 PHRASING

SOUND ADVICE

Discuss with students how to execute phrases that are marked with "n.b." (no breath).

135   PHRASING

SOUND ADVICE

▶ Percussion: Remind students to dampen on rests that are not marked to let ring.

136 ARTICULATION

SOUND ADVICE

Have students work toward vivid contrasts of articulation.

▶ Mallets: Use finger dampening for the marcato pitches.

137 **DYNAMICS**

SOUND ADVICE

Have students work toward vivid contrasts of dynamics.

138 **ETUDE**

139   **ETUDE**

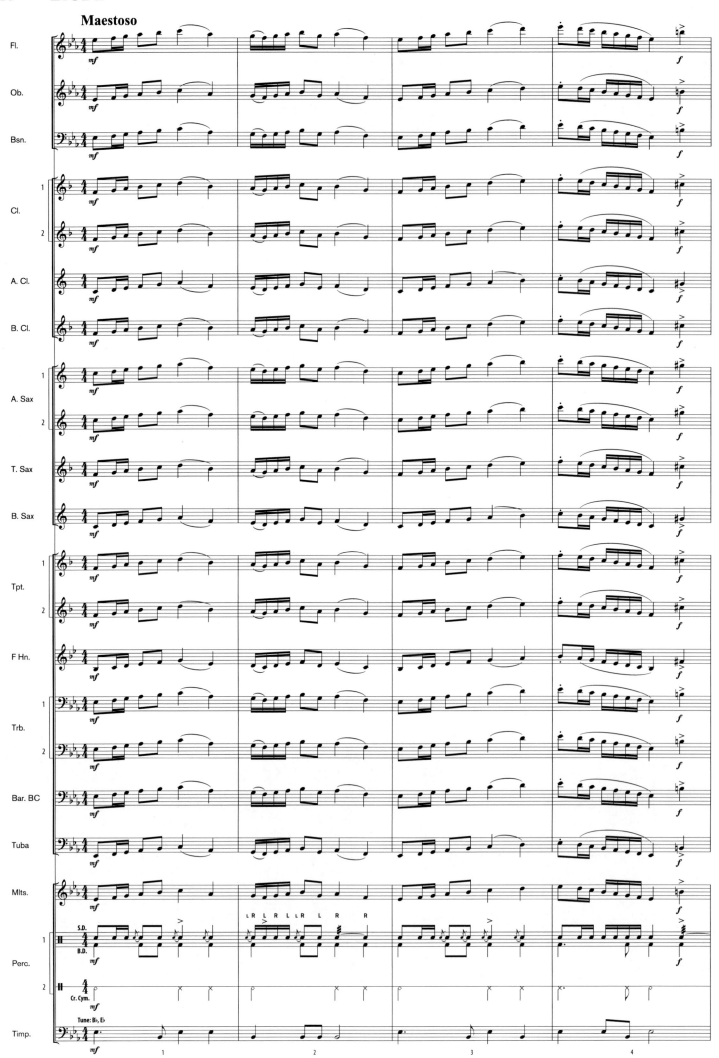

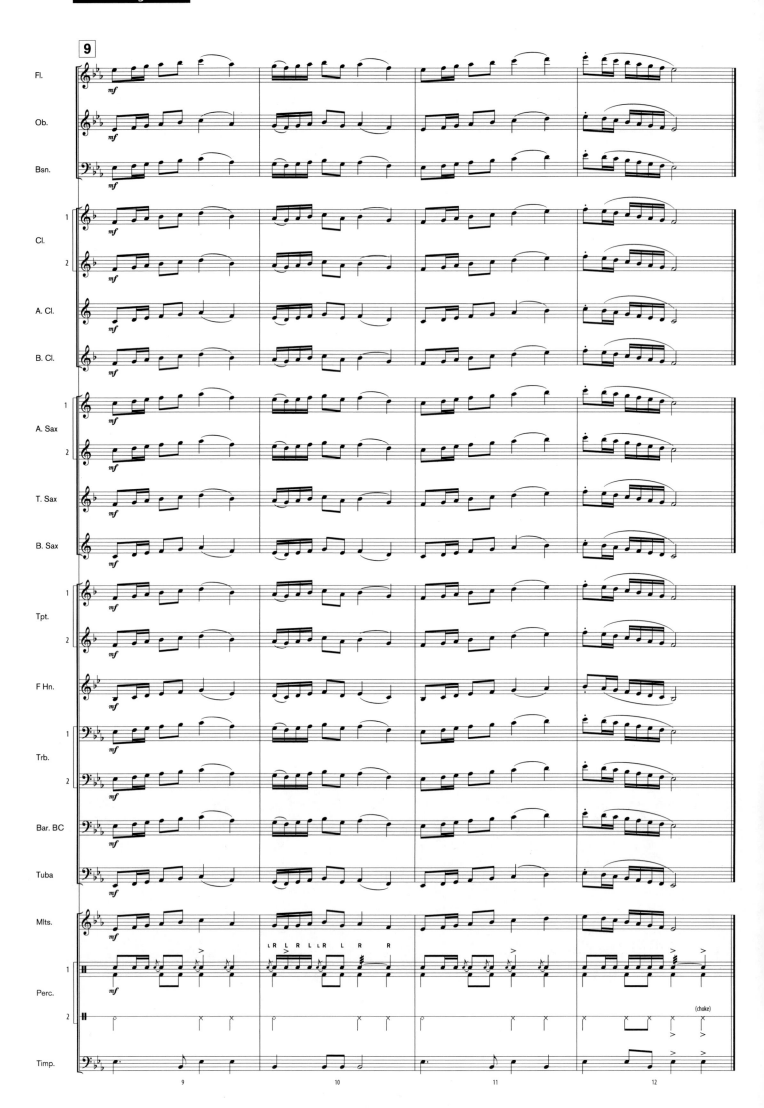

140 **CHORALE**

Todd Stalter

141 **CHORALE**

Randall D. Standridge (ASCAP)

142 **CONCERT E♭ MAJOR SCALE & CHORALE**

Chris M. Bernotas (ASCAP)

143 **CHORALE**

Michael Story (ASCAP)

144 **CHORALE**

Andrew Boysen, Jr.

145 **CHORALE**

Robert Sheldon

146 **CHORALE**

Ralph Ford (ASCAP)

147 **CHORALE**

Rossano Galante

148 **CHORALE**

Chris M. Bernotas (ASCAP)

149 **CHORALE**

Randall D. Standridge (ASCAP)

Concert C Minor

150   PASSING THE TONIC

SOUND ADVICE

▶ Trumpet: Discuss with students when to use the third valve slide and its importance.

151 **BREATHING AND LONG TONES**

SOUND ADVICE

▶ Snare Drum: This exercise incorporates the lesson 25 rudiment.

152 CONCERT C NATURAL MINOR SCALE

SOUND ADVICE

▶ Snare Drum: Be sure to make your 9-stroke rolls even.

153 CONCERT C HARMONIC AND MELODIC MINOR SCALES

SOUND ADVICE

▶ Percussion: This exercise provides a great opportunity to practice alternate stickings.

154 SCALE PATTERN

SOUND ADVICE

Have students master this exercise at a slow tempo and then gradually increase the speed to develop technical facility.

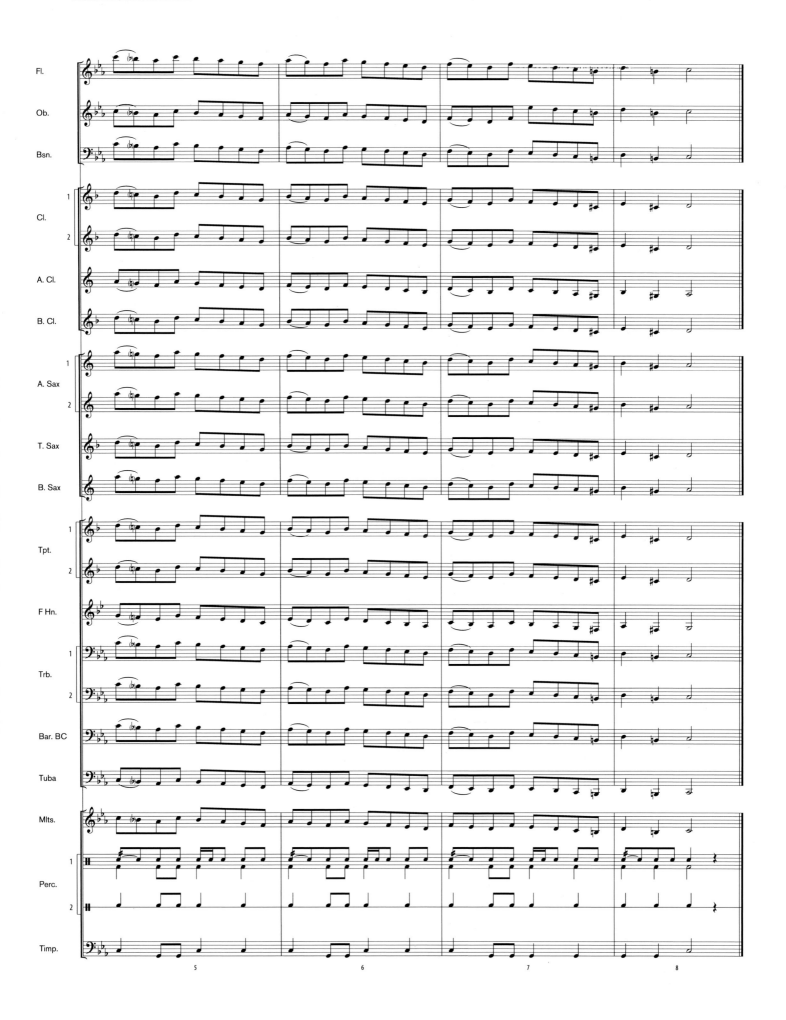

155   CONCERT C CHROMATIC SCALE

SOUND ADVICE

▶ Clarinet and Bass Clarinet: Remind students to use the chromatic F♯ fingering for this exercise.

▶ Alto Clarinet: Remind students to use the chromatic B and F♯ fingerings for this exercise.

156   **FLEXIBILITY**

SOUND ADVICE

Remind students not to clip short the last note of a slur.

157 FLEXIBILITY

SOUND ADVICE

▶ Brass: Remind students to play higher notes by keeping a firm embouchure as they increase the speed of the airstream.

158 ARPEGGIOS

SOUND ADVICE
This exercise could also be performed with any number of students sustaining the first note as a drone to further develop intonation skills.

159   ARPEGGIOS

SOUND ADVICE

Remind students not to clip short notes before a rest.

160   INTERVALS

SOUND ADVICE

▶ Trumpet: Remind students the importance of adjusting the pitch with the third valve slide. Students can leave it out for this whole exercise.

161 INTERVALS

SOUND ADVICE

This exercise uses the harmonic form of the minor scale as it ascends and the natural form as it descends.

162 **BALANCE AND INTONATION: DIATONIC HARMONY**

SOUND ADVICE

▶ Snare Drum: This exercise incorporates the single stroke seven rudiment.

163 **BALANCE AND INTONATION: MOVING CHORD TONES**

SOUND ADVICE

▶ Percussion: Discuss with students how some rhythms sound the same, even though they can be written differently.

BALANCE AND INTONATION: LAYERED TUNING

SOUND ADVICE
Have students work toward melding their sound into that of the ensemble.

165 BALANCE AND INTONATION: FAMILY BALANCE

SOUND ADVICE
Have students perform this exercise using a variety of articulations and dynamics.

166 EXPANDING INTERVALS: DOWNWARD IN TRIADS

SOUND ADVICE

▶ Trumpet 2: Remind students to adjust the pitch on the D and D♭ using the third valve slide.

167 EXPANDING INTERVALS: UPWARD IN TRIADS

SOUND ADVICE

▶ Percussion 2: Be aware that the performer is required to switch between using felt mallets and sticks.

168   **RHYTHM**

SOUND ADVICE

▶ Trumpet: Remind students to keep their left thumb horizontally across the valve casing, rather than sticking straight up.

▶ Timpani: Make certain students dampen on the rests

169 **RHYTHM**

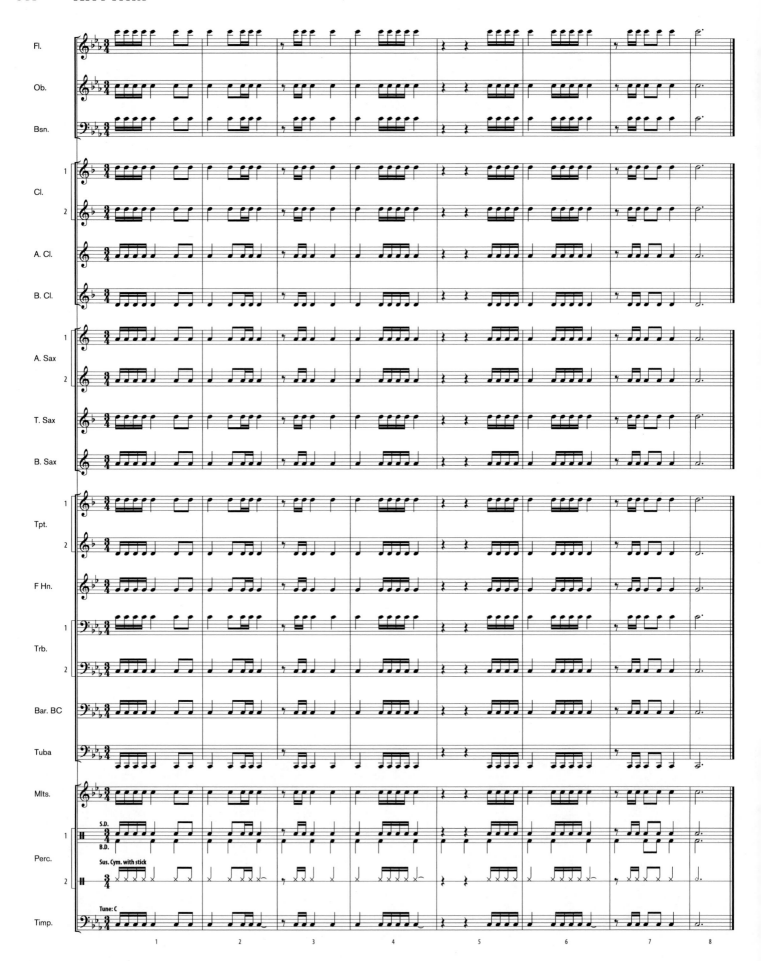

SOUND ADVICE
▶ Woodwinds: Remind students of the importance of soaking reeds before playing and drying reeds out after playing.

170 **RHYTHM**

SOUND ADVICE

▶ Snare Drum: This exercise incorporates the double paradiddle.

171 **RHYTHMIC SUBDIVISION**

SOUND ADVICE

▶ Brass: Players should consider trying different syllables, such as "daw" or "taw," to help achieve lower notes, and "dee" or "tee" to help achieve higher notes.

172 **RHYTHMIC SUBDIVISION**

SOUND ADVICE

Remind students to completely depress keys or valves, and move slides quickly before making a sound.

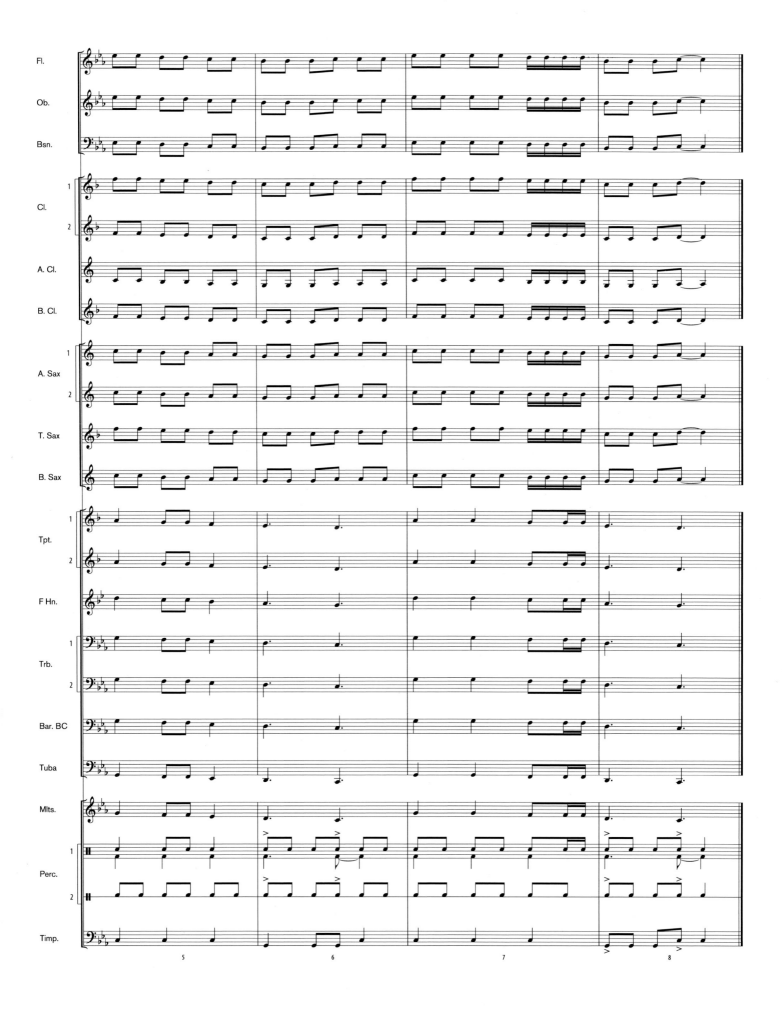

173 ARTICULATION AND DYNAMICS

SOUND ADVICE

▶ Brass: Remind students to use as little pressure against the lips as possible.

▶ Percussion: Remind students to dampen on the rests and notes with a staccato marking.

174   **ETUDE**

175 # CHORALE

Randall D. Standridge (ASCAP)

176 **CHORALE**

Roland Barrett

177 **CONCERT C MINOR SCALE & CHORALE**

Chris M. Bernotas (ASCAP)

178

From the Gotha Psalter, 1726
Harmonized by J.S. Bach (1685–1750)
Arranged by Todd Stalter

CHORALE: MEINES LEBENS LETZTE ZEIT

179 **CHORALE**

Rossano Galante

Concert F Major

180   **PASSING THE TONIC**

SOUND ADVICE

Help students achieve a blended and balanced sound.

181 BREATHING AND LONG TONES

SOUND ADVICE

Suggest that students push the airstream faster for upward leaps in pitch.

▶ Horn: Slur open on the F side of the horn from C to G without hitting the E in between. Students should have good support, firm embouchure, and perhaps use syllables "taw-ee" to make the leap and "tee-aw" to go back down again.

▶ Percussion: Discuss with students how the accents outline a dotted quarter note. $\frac{3}{4}$ time can sometimes act like $\frac{6}{8}$ time.

182   CONCERT F MAJOR SCALE

SOUND ADVICE

▶ Snare Drum: This exercise incorporates the 4-stroke ruff.

183 SCALE PATTERN

SOUND ADVICE

▶ Flute: Encourage students to work for a beautiful tone as they ascend to the high G.

▶ Trumpet: Encourage students to work for a beautiful tone as they ascend to the high A.

▶ Trombone: Encourage students to work for a beautiful tone as they ascend to the high G.

▶ Baritone: Encourage students to work for a beautiful tone as they ascend to the high G.

184 SCALE PATTERN

SOUND ADVICE
▶ Brass: If students have difficulty playing lower notes, have them relax the embouchure slightly, while maintaining a steady airstream, and experiment with various syllables, such as "ah," "tah," "oh," or "toh."

185 **CONCERT F CHROMATIC SCALE**

SOUND ADVICE
▶ Clarinet, Alto Clarinet and Bass Clarinet: Remember to use chromatic alternate fingerings.

186 **FLEXIBILITY**

SOUND ADVICE

▶ Brass: Remind players to keep their embouchures firm, but relaxed, when playing large downward leaps.

▶ Horn: Try this exercise entirely on the F side. Be careful of not hitting the false B♭ (third line) or the first line E. Change notes at the last possible second, and keep good support and a firm embouchure. Using the syllables "tee," "ahh," and "aww," from high to low, respectively may help

187   **FLEXIBILITY**

SOUND ADVICE

▶ Horn: To play in the lower range, it may help to use the syllable "taw," which will lower the jaw slightly.

188 **ARPEGGIOS**

SOUND ADVICE

▶ Horn: Make certain students have their hands in the bell correctly.

189 **ARPEGGIOS**

SOUND ADVICE

To help students develop improvisation skills, have them improvise using the pitches in this exercise

▶ Percussion 2: Discuss with students the markings for closed and open playing.

▶ Timpani: Discuss how to dampen for staccato markings.

190 **INTERVALS**

SOUND ADVICE

Challenge students to see how many notes they can play with one breath.

191 **BALANCE AND INTONATION: DIATONIC HARMONY**

SOUND ADVICE

Discuss with students the appropriate place to breathe in this exercise.

192 **BALANCE AND INTONATION: FAMILY BALANCE**

SOUND ADVICE

Discuss with students how they can dovetail their attacks and releases to work toward a unified ensemble sound.

193 **BALANCE AND INTONATION: LAYERED TUNING**

SOUND ADVICE

▶ Brass and Woodwinds: Suggest that students not use lip gloss, lipstick or lip balm before playing their instruments.

Student Page 27

194 BALANCE AND INTONATION: MOVING CHORD TONES

SOUND ADVICE

This exercise could also be performed with any number of students sustaining the first note as a drone to further develop intonation skills.

▶ Horn: This entire exercise can be played on the F side open. Be careful not to hit the first line E or the third line (false) B♭ when going from note to note.

195   BALANCE AND INTONATION: SHIFTING CHORD QUALITIES

SOUND ADVICE

Have half of the students sing or hum this exercise, while the other half plays.

This may be a good place to discuss enharmonic tones with students.

▶ Timpani: Use your ear to tune the drum down in half steps.

196 **EXPANDING INTERVALS: DOWNWARD IN PARALLEL FIFTHS**

SOUND ADVICE

▶ Horn: Make sure each student has the bell aimed off to the right side, rather than faced directly into his or her stomach.

197   **EXPANDING INTERVALS: UPWARD IN PARALLEL FIFTHS**

SOUND ADVICE

▶ Trumpet 2: Remind students to be sure to use the 3rd valve slide to adjust the pitch on the note D.

198 RHYTHM

SOUND ADVICE

Have students perform this exercise using a variety of articulations and dynamics.

199   **RHYTHM**

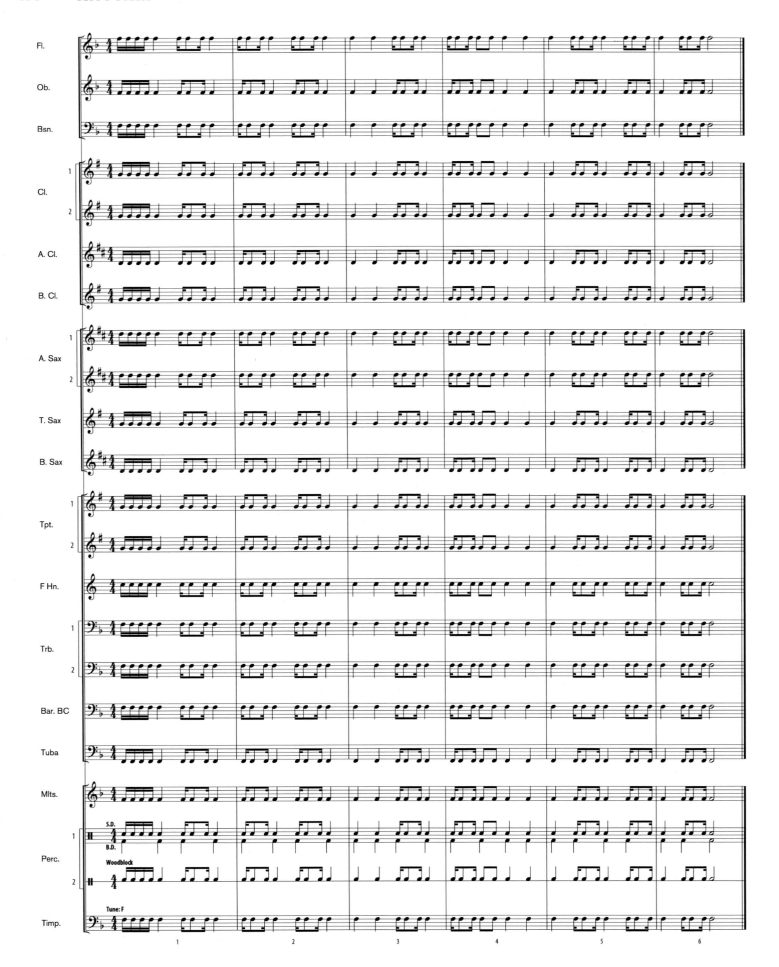

SOUND ADVICE

▶ Flute: Remind students to work toward clear and precise tonguing, rather than a "hooting" sound.

200   RHYTHM

SOUND ADVICE

Be insistent about students keeping their feet flat on the floor with their backs away from the chairs.

201 **RHYTHMIC SUBDIVISION**

SOUND ADVICE
Remind students not to pinch their embouchures.

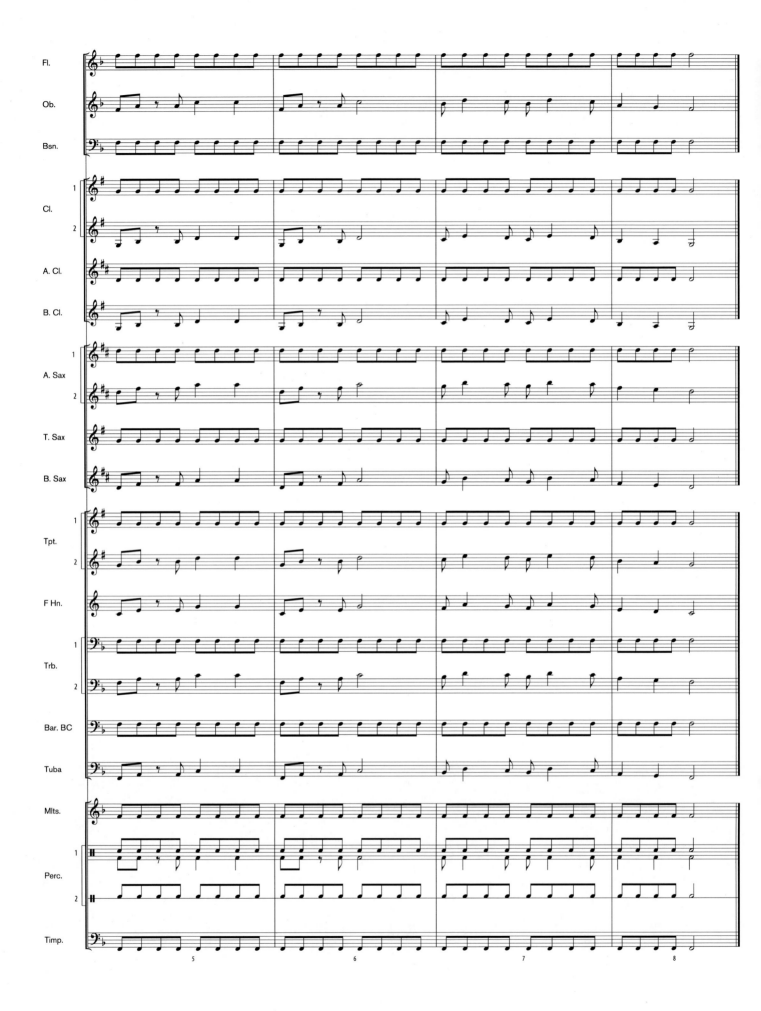

202 **RHYTHMIC SUBDIVISION**

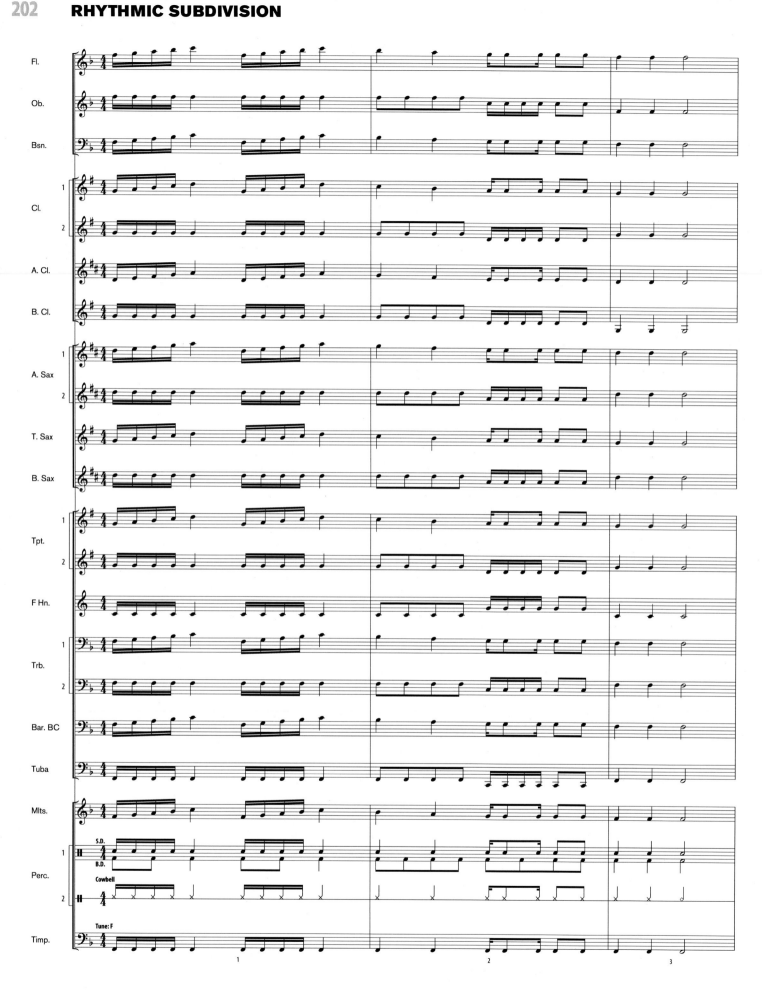

SOUND ADVICE

Ask students to master this exercise at faster tempos to improve their technical facility.

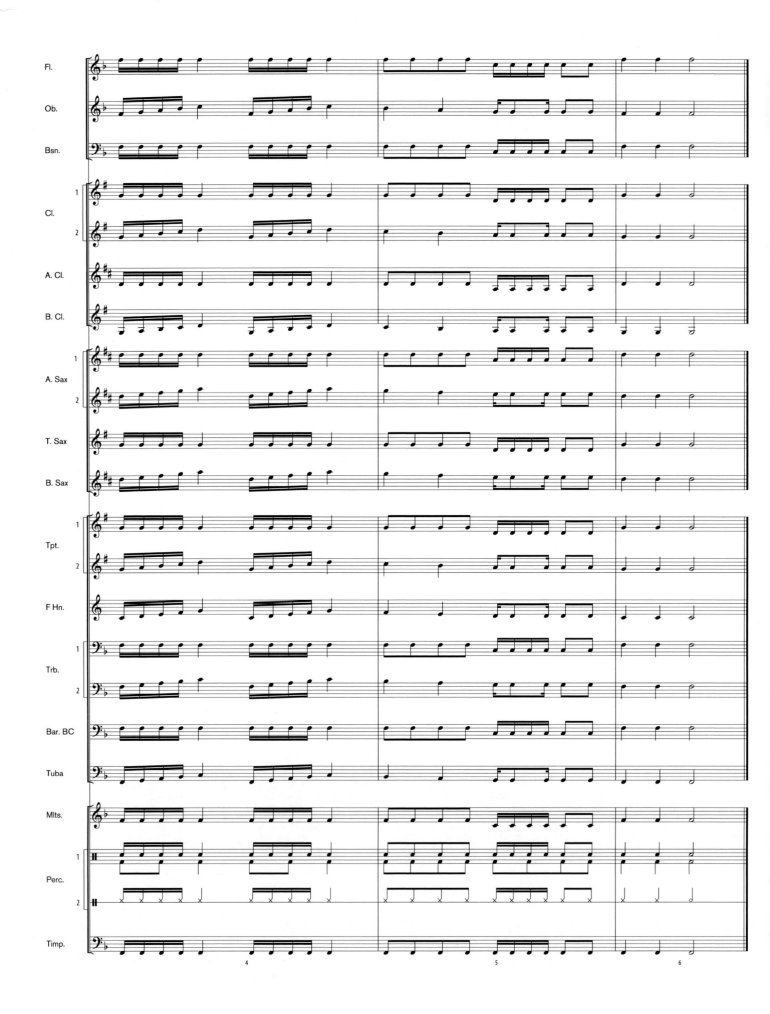

203 **ARTICULATION AND DYNAMICS**

SOUND ADVICE

Have students work toward vivid contrasts of articulation and dynamics.

204 **ETUDE**

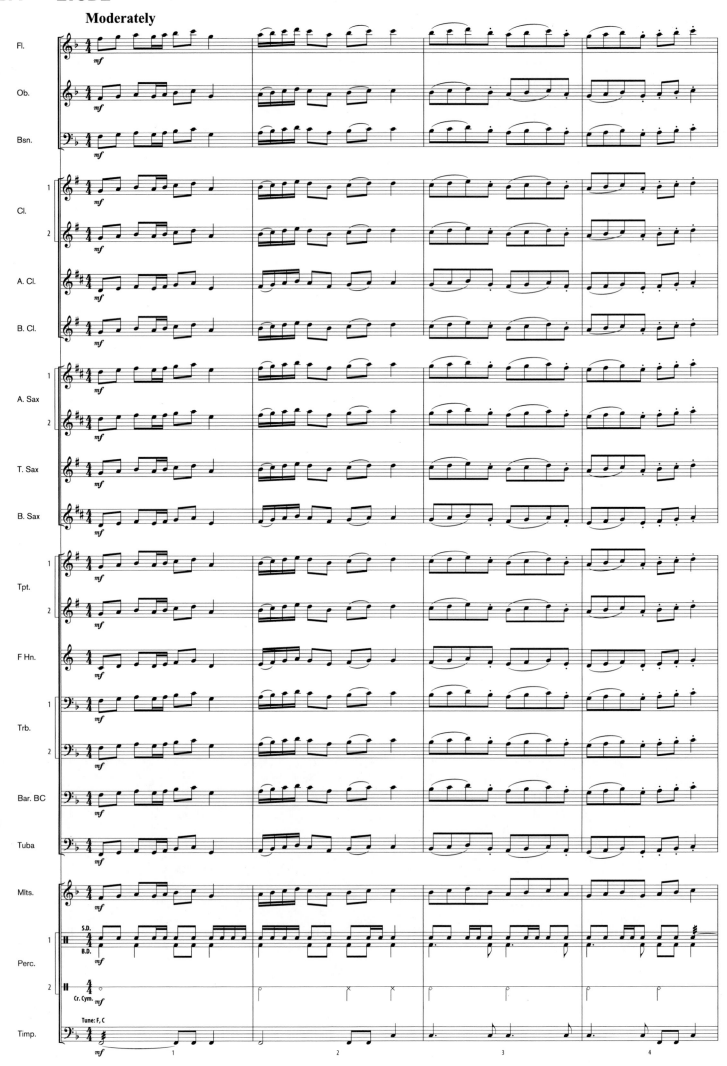

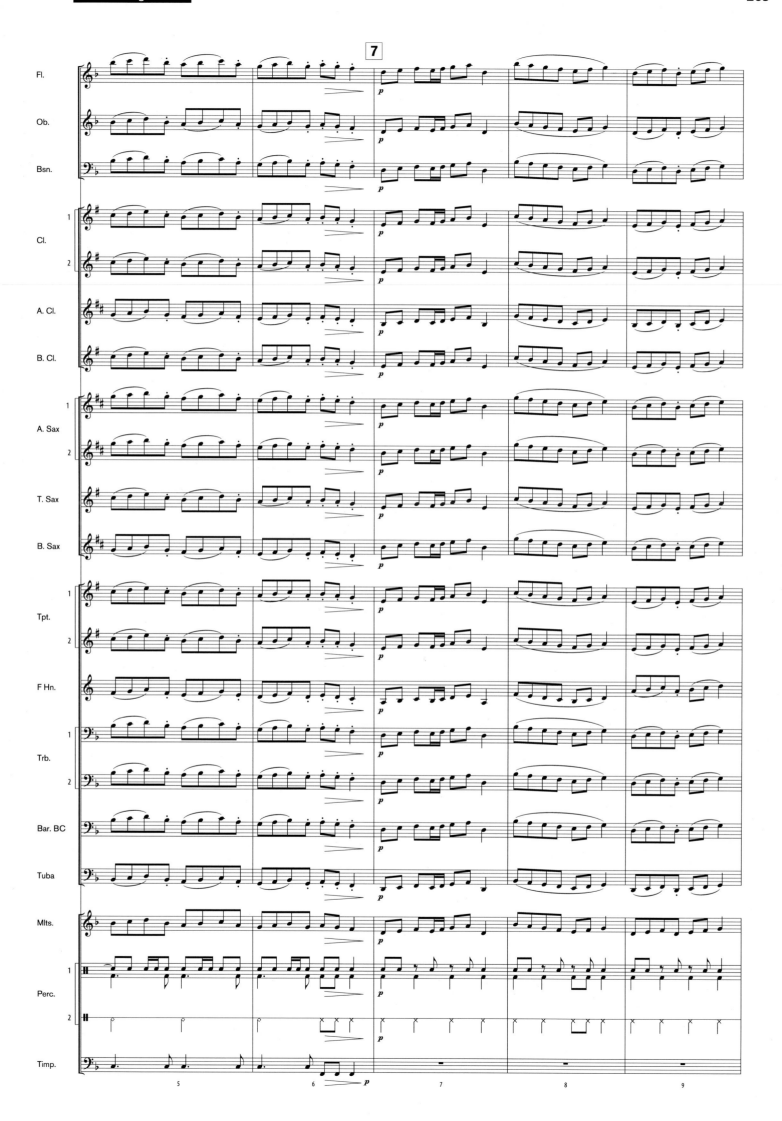

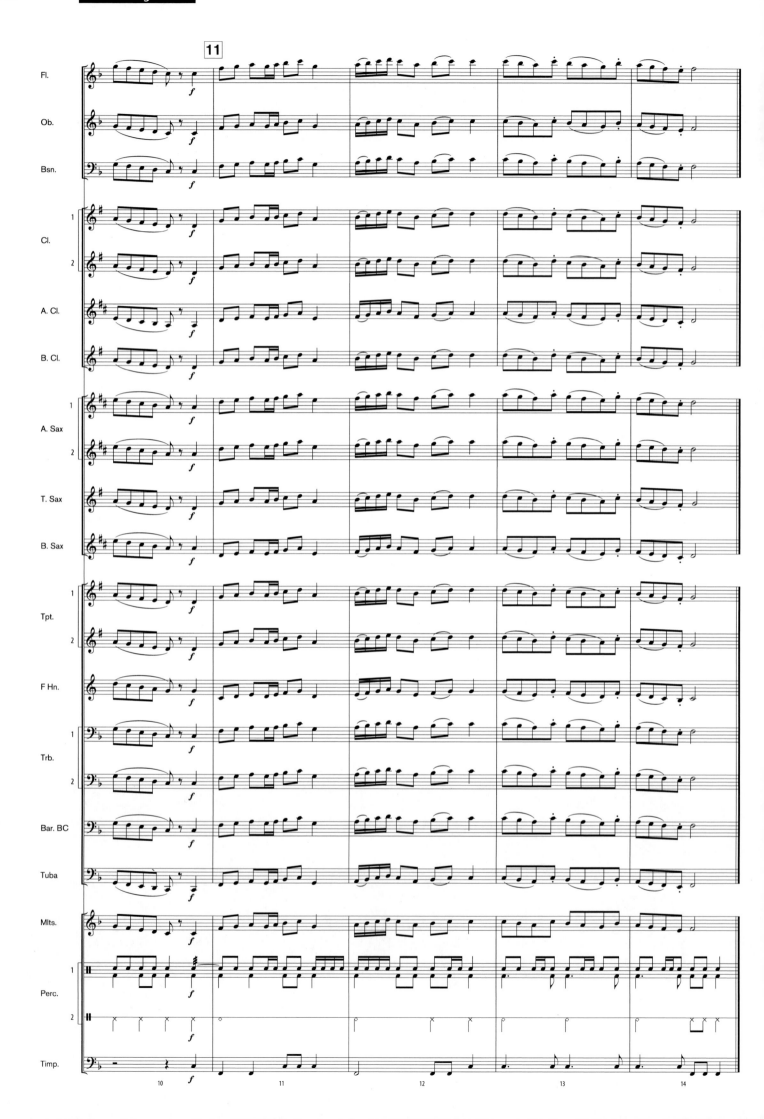

205 **CHORALE: OVERTURE 1812**

Pyotr Ilyich Tchaikovsky
Arranged by Michael Story (ASCAP)

206 **CHORALE**

Randall D. Standridge (ASCAP)

207 **CONCERT F MAJOR SCALE & CHORALE**

Chris M. Bernotas (ASCAP)

208 **CHORALE**

Rossano Galante

209 **CHORALE**

Ralph Ford (ASCAP)

Concert D Minor

210   PASSING THE TONIC

SOUND ADVICE

Discuss with students the appropriate place to breathe in this exercise.

Remind students to pay as much attention to the releases of their notes as they do to their attacks.

211 BREATHING AND LONG TONES

SOUND ADVICE
Remind students of the importance of good posture and playing position.

212 ## CONCERT D NATURAL MINOR SCALE

SOUND ADVICE
▶ Snare Drum: Remind students to work toward even 9-stroke rolls.

213 CONCERT D HARMONIC AND MELODIC MINOR SCALES

SOUND ADVICE
Remind students to move fingers, valves, keys or slides quickly and firmly.

214 SCALE PATTERN

SOUND ADVICE
Remind students to keep fingers close to the keys or valves for quicker, more precise playing.

215 SCALE PATTERN

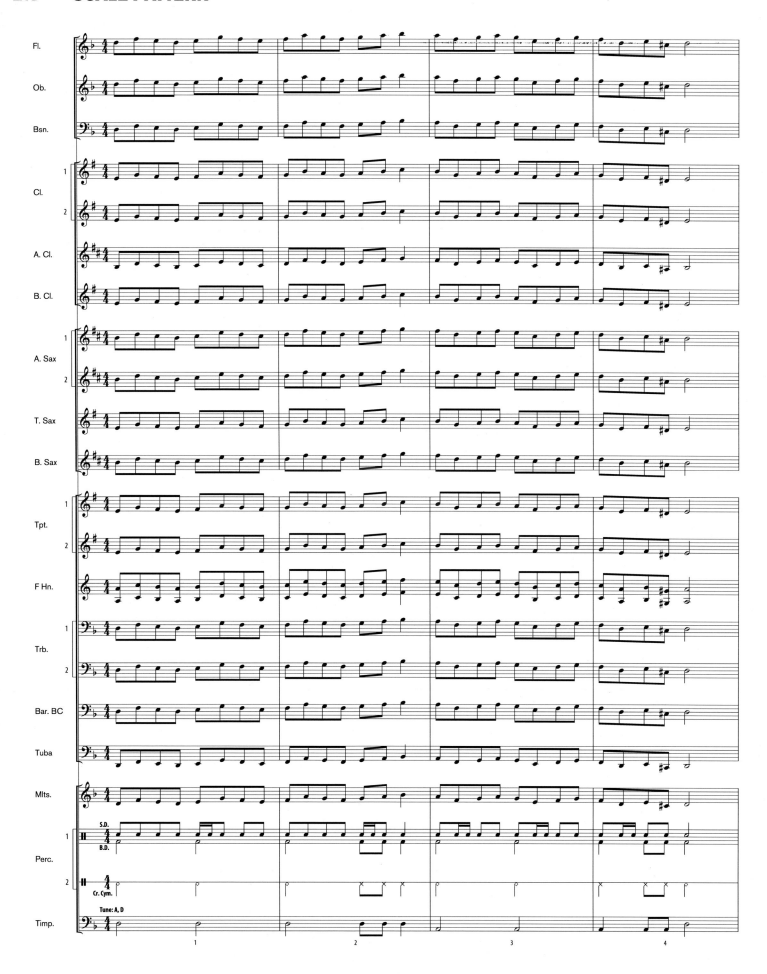

SOUND ADVICE

Experiment with different articulations to provide variety for this exercise.

216 **CONCERT D CHROMATIC SCALE**

SOUND ADVICE

▶ Clarinet, Alto Clarinet and Bass Clarinet: Remember to use chromatic alternate fingerings.

217   **FLEXIBILITY**

SOUND ADVICE

▶ Snare Drum: This exercise incorporates the flam drag.

218   **FLEXIBILITY**

SOUND ADVICE

▶ Brass: Remind students to use as little pressure against the lips as possible.

219 **ARPEGGIOS**

SOUND ADVICE

Encourage students to maintain a consistent volume as they ascend and descend through various registers.

220 **ARPEGGIOS**

SOUND ADVICE

Discuss with students the appropriate place to breathe in this exercise.

221   **INTERVALS**

SOUND ADVICE

▶ Brass: Remind students to play higher notes by keeping a firm embouchure as they increase the speed of the airstream.

222

BALANCE AND INTONATION: DIATONIC HARMONY

SOUND ADVICE

Have half of the students sing or hum this exercise, while the other half plays.

223 ## BALANCE AND INTONATION: FAMILY BALANCE

SOUND ADVICE
Encourage students to listen to each other while playing to develop a blended and balanced ensemble sound.

224 **BALANCE AND INTONATION: LAYERED TUNING**

SOUND ADVICE

Stress the importance of deep, full breaths to sustain long durations.

225   **BALANCE AND INTONATON: MOVING CHORD TONES**

SOUND ADVICE

Have some brass students buzz this exercise on their mouthpiece, while other brass and/or woodwind students play it.

226 **EXPANDING INTERVALS: DOWNWARD IN TRIADS**

SOUND ADVICE

▶ Clarinet 1: Keep your right hand down for the first four measures when descending.

▶ Alto Clarinet: Use the chromatic B for the first measure

▶ Percussion: This exercise incorporates the single stroke four rudiment.

227 **EXPANDING INTERVALS: UPWARD IN TRIADS**

SOUND ADVICE

Remind students not to clip the last note of a slur.

228 **RHYTHM**

SOUND ADVICE

Have students write in the counting and then clap the exercise before actually playing it.

229 **RHYTHM**

SOUND ADVICE
▶ Snare Drum: This exercise incorporates the 7-stroke roll.

230   **RHYTHM**

SOUND ADVICE
Have half the class conduct this exercise, while the other half claps or plays it.

231   RHYTHMIC SUBDIVISION

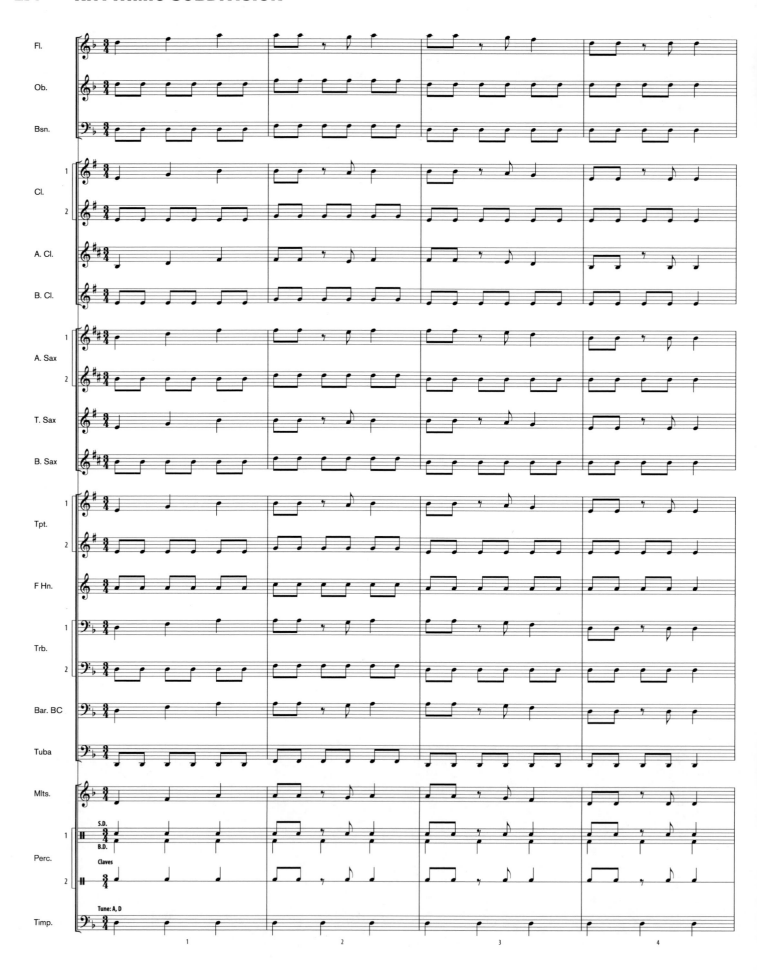

SOUND ADVICE

Remind students that the second of a pair of eighth notes should not be clipped or rushed.

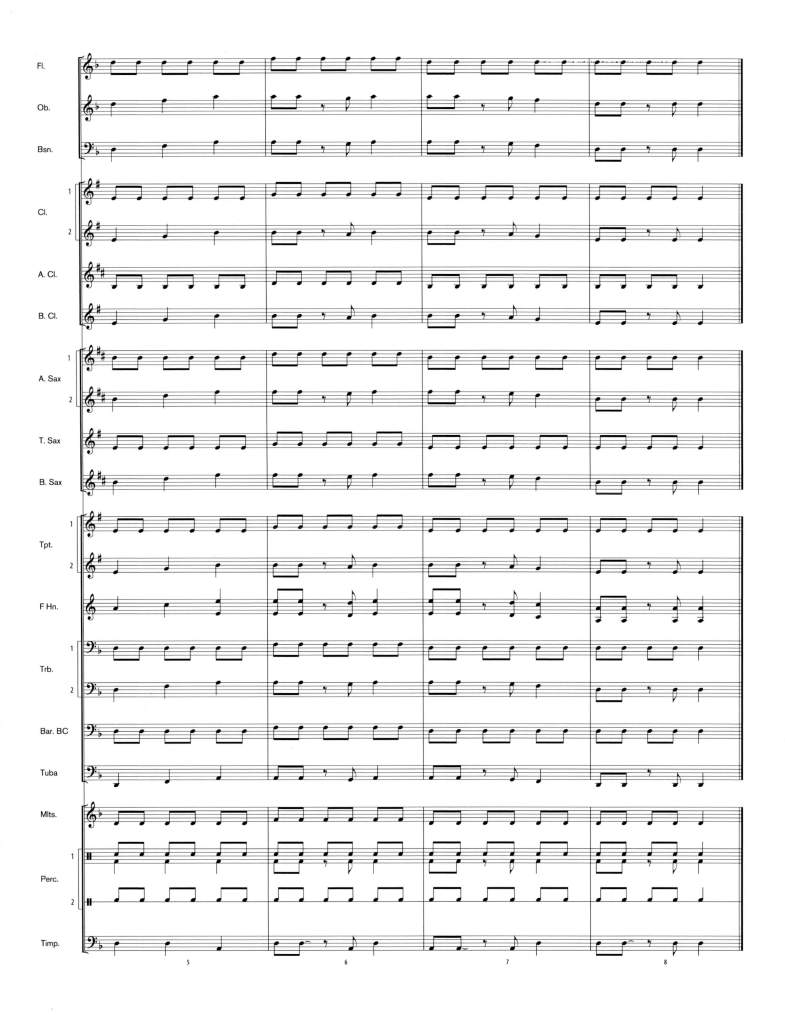

232 **RHYTHMIC SUBDIVISION**

SOUND ADVICE

Have students be mindful of the rhythmic subdivision to prevent the rushing of syncopated rhythms.

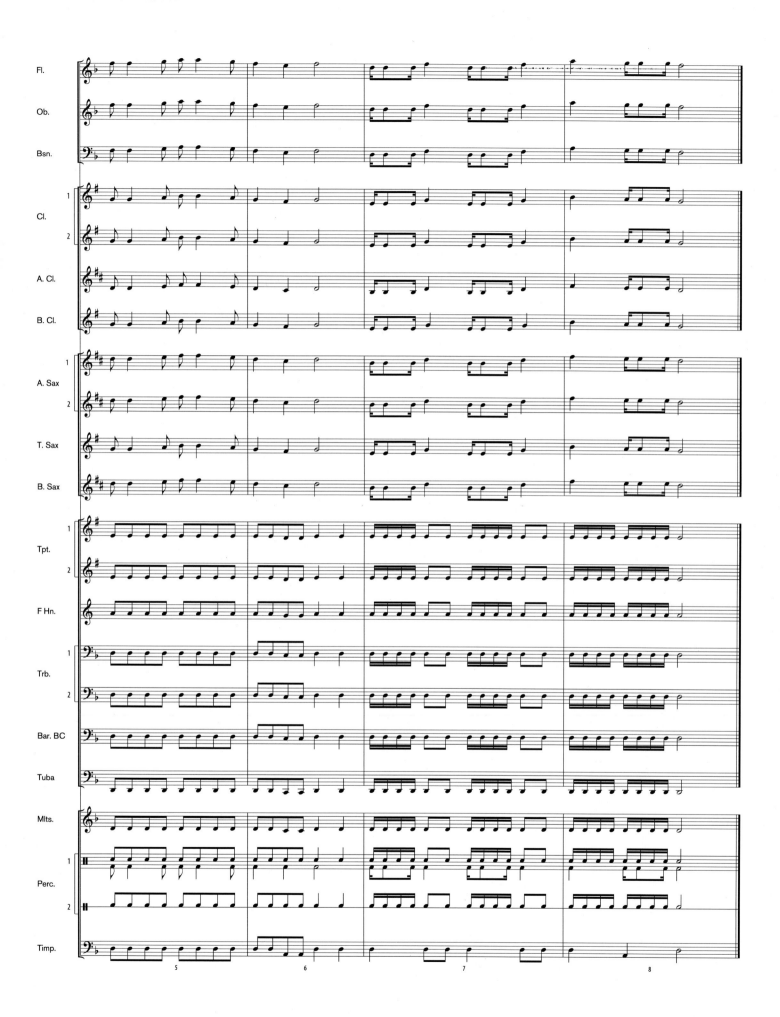

233 ARTICULATION AND DYNAMICS

SOUND ADVICE

Remind students that crescendos and decrescendos must be performed in a gradual manner.

234 **ETUDE**

235 **CHORALE**

Roland Barrett

236 CHORALE

Andrew Boysen, Jr.

237 **CONCERT D MINOR SCALE & CHORALE**

Chris M. Bernotas (ASCAP)

238 **CHORALE**

Robert Sheldon

239 **CHORALE: PSALM 33**

From the Genevan Psalter
Harmonized by Claude Goudimel (c. 1520–1572)
Arranged/Edited by Todd Stalter

Concert A♭ Major

240 **PASSING THE TONIC**

SOUND ADVICE

Remind students to pay as much attention to the releases of the notes as they do to the attacks.

241 BREATHING AND LONG TONES

SOUND ADVICE

Encourage students to exhale before inhaling to promote deep breathing.

242 **CONCERT A♭ MAJOR SCALE**

SOUND ADVICE

▶ Snare Drum: This exercise incorporates the 7-stroke roll.

243 **SCALE PATTERN**

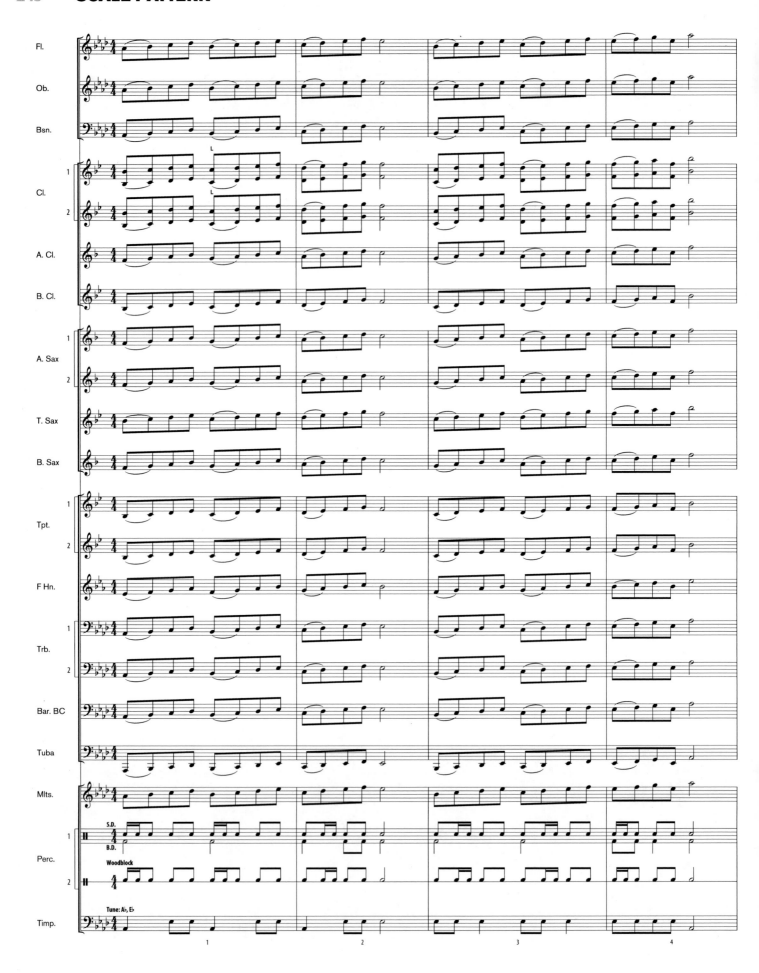

SOUND ADVICE

Have students practice this exercise with a variety of articulation patterns.

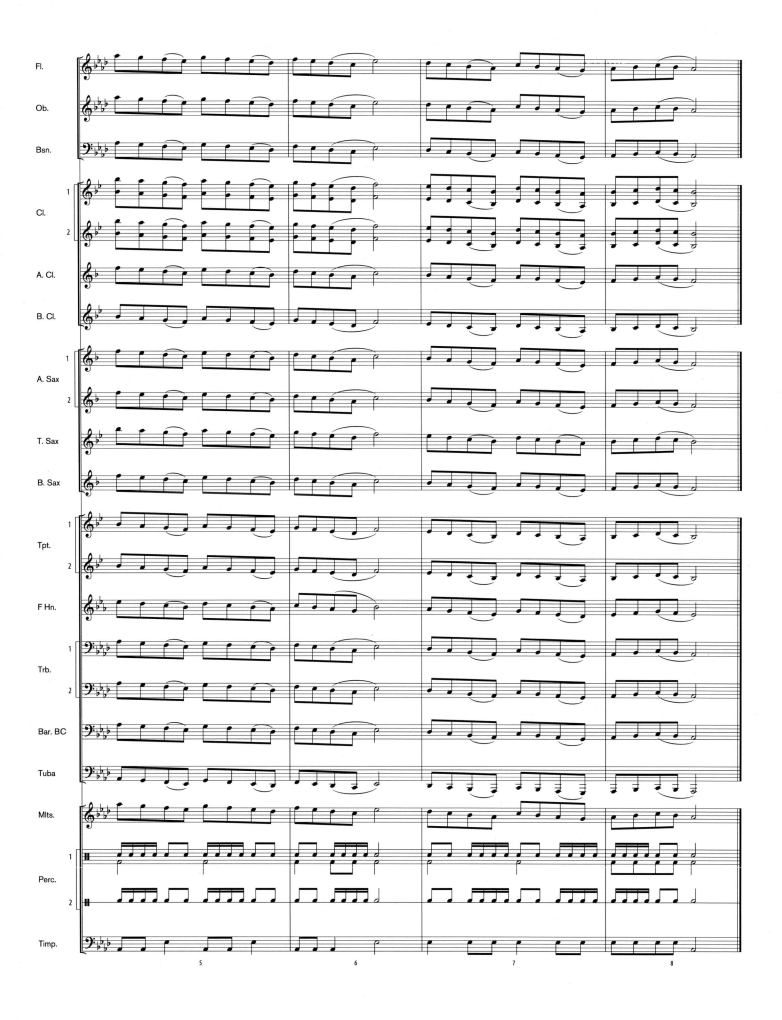

244 **SCALE PATTERN**

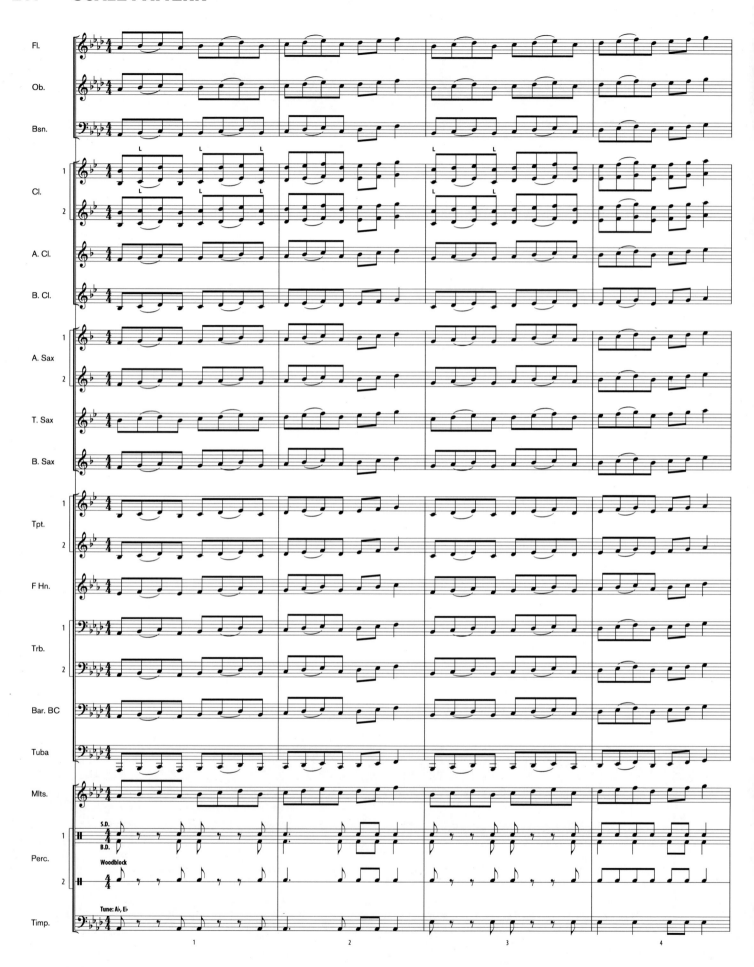

SOUND ADVICE

Have students master this exercise at a slow tempo and then gradually increase the speed to develop technical facility.

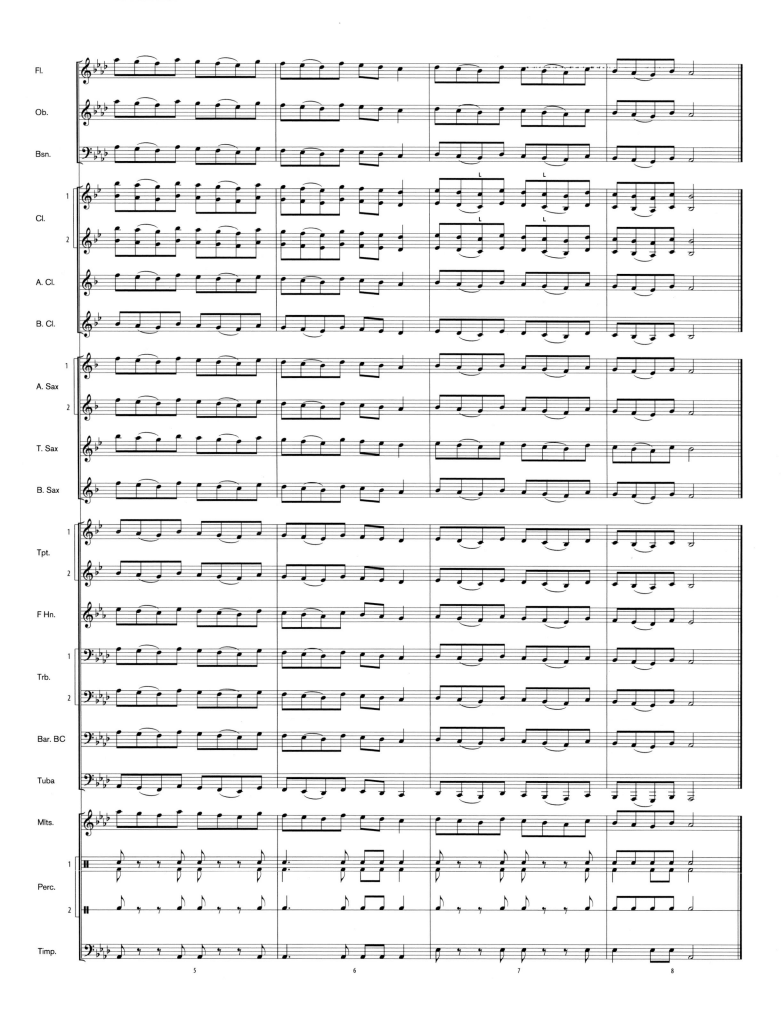

245

CONCERT A♭ CHROMATIC SCALE

SOUND ADVICE

▶ Clarinet, Alto Clarinet and Bass Clarinet: Remember to use chromatic alternate fingerings.

246 **FLEXIBILITY**

SOUND ADVICE

This exercise includes upward and downward leaps. This would be an excellent opportunity to discuss how embouchure, airstream and tongue position make this possible.

▶ Snare Drum: This exercise incorporates the 7-stroke roll.

247 **FLEXIBILITY**

SOUND ADVICE

▶ Clarinet, Alto Clarinet and Bass Clarinet: Guard against students holding the instrument either against their torso or too far out in front of them.

▶ Horn: This entire exercise can be played on the B♭ side of the horn, T1.

248 ARPEGGIOS

SOUND ADVICE

Remind students to keep their shoulders relaxed, especially when moving upward in this exercise.

▶ Horn: This entire exercise can be played on the B♭ side of the horn, T1, as an exercise for fingers on the B♭ side.

249 **ARPEGGIOS**

SOUND ADVICE

▶ Trombone: Encourage students to move the slide quickly between positions, waiting until the last moment before moving between notes.

250 INTERVALS

SOUND ADVICE

▶ Brass: Remind students to play higher notes by keeping a firm embouchure as they increase the speed of the airstream.

251   **BALANCE AND INTONATION: DIATONIC HARMONY**

SOUND ADVICE

Have half of the students sing or hum this exercise, while the other half plays.

252 **BALANCE AND INTONATION: FAMILY BALANCE**

SOUND ADVICE

▶ Snare Drum: This exercise incorporates the single ratamacue

253   BALANCE AND INTONATION: LAYERED TUNING

SOUND ADVICE

▶ Flute: Remind students that their instruments should be approximately parallel to the floor rather than pointed downward. They should also be reminded to never rest their right arms or elbows on the backs of their chairs.

254

BALANCE AND INTONATION: MOVING CHORD TONES

SOUND ADVICE

▶ Clarinet, Alto Clarinet and Bass Clarinet: Students may achieve a darker and richer tone by dropping their bottom lip down on the reed an eighth of an inch more, as they bring the bell of the instrument a bit closer to their bodies. This placement promotes greater reed vibration, better chin position and good playing posture.

255   **EXPANDING INTERVALS: DOWNWARD IN PARALLEL FIFTHS**

SOUND ADVICE

▶ Trumpet, Baritone/Euphonium and Tuba: This would be a good time to remind students to use their fingertips to depress the valves to promote better technique.

256 EXPANDING INTERVALS: UPWARD IN PARALLEL THIRDS

SOUND ADVICE

▶ Woodwinds (except Flute): Encourage students to always have at least one extra reed available. Many teachers encourage students to have at least three reeds and rotate their use every day.

257   **RHYTHM**

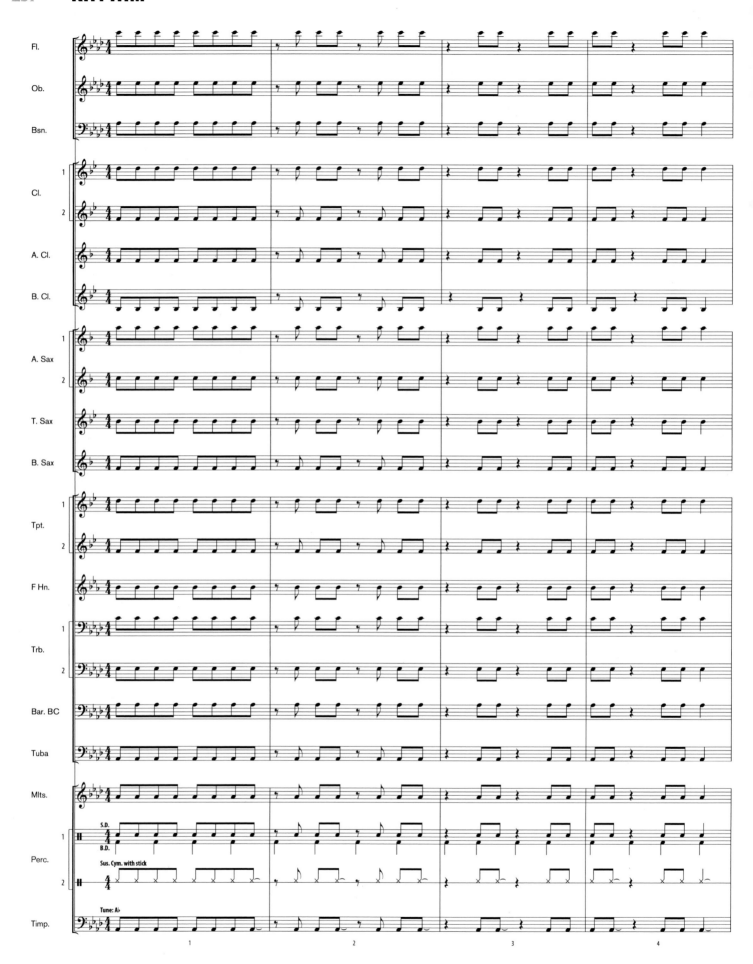

SOUND ADVICE

Encourage students to count with subdivisions to avoid rushing in this exercise.

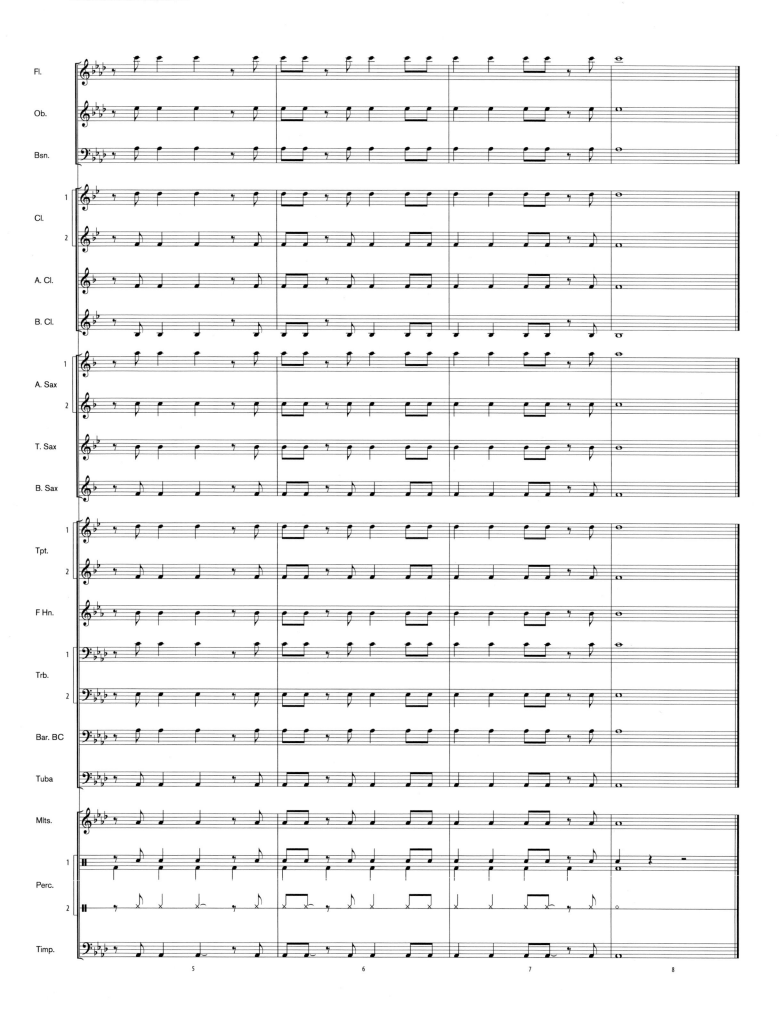

258 **RHYTHM**

SOUND ADVICE

Have half the ensemble clap the rhythm of this tune, while the other half plays, then vice versa.

259   **RHYTHM**

SOUND ADVICE

For additional practice have the ensemble perform this exercise in 6 and in 2.

260 RHYTHMIC SUBDIVISION

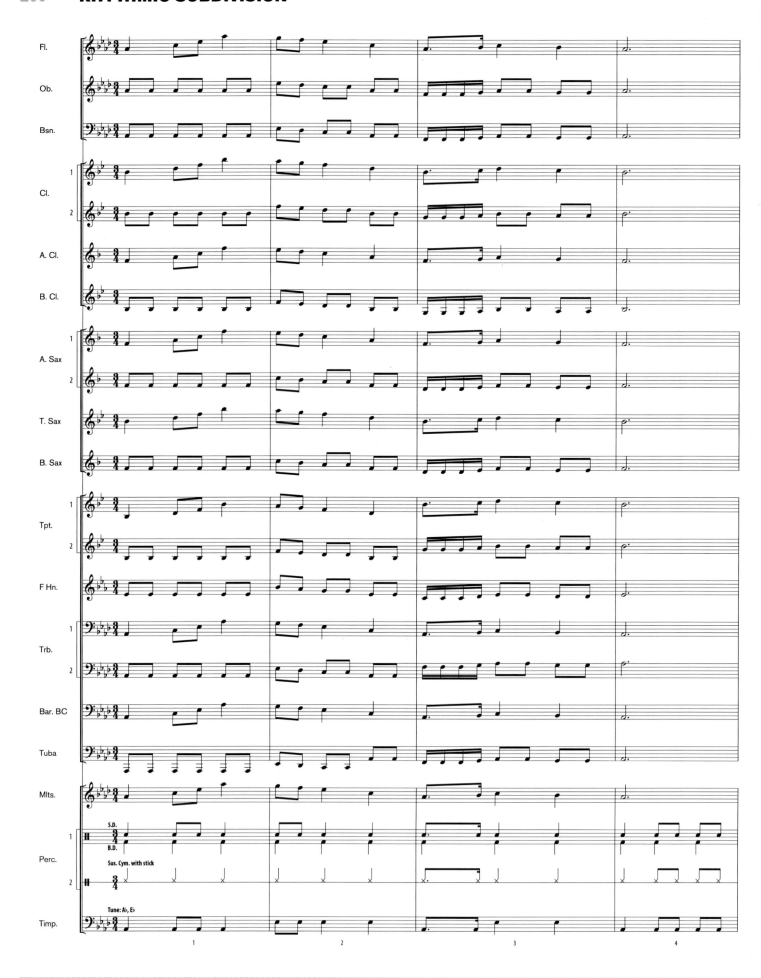

SOUND ADVICE

▶ Clarinets: This would be a great place to use the 1+1 fingering for high B♭.

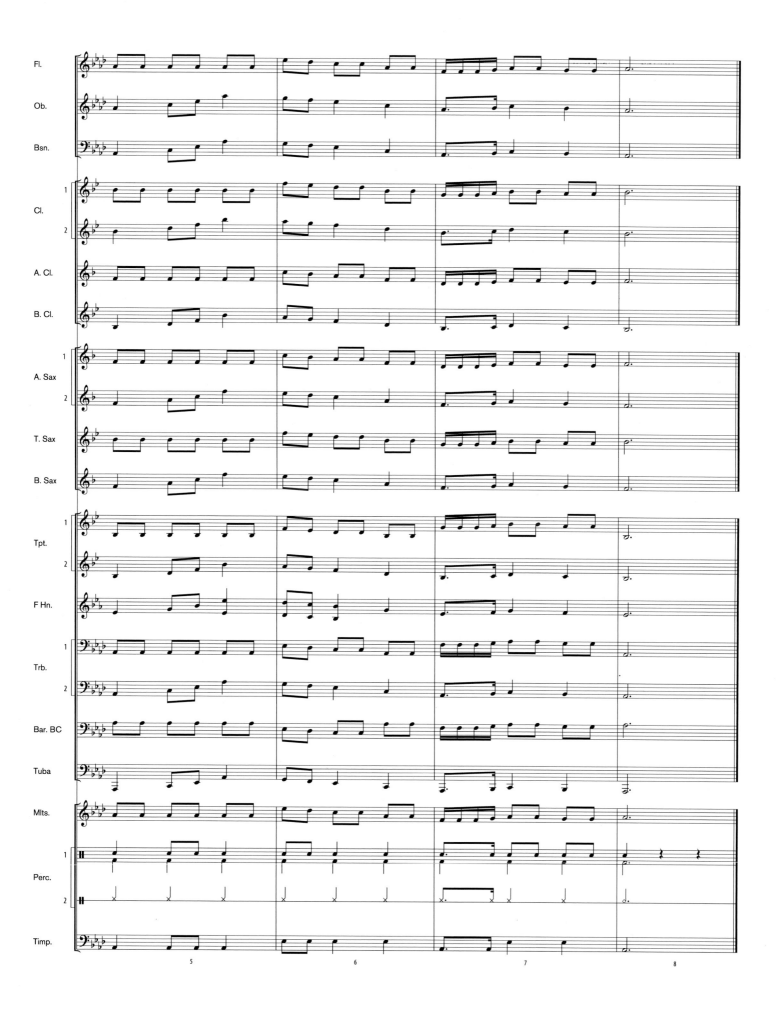

261 **RHYTHMIC SUBDIVISION**

SOUND ADVICE

When playing the melodic portion of this exercise make certain to execute the eighth notes for their full duration, so as to avoid rushing the tempo.

262 **DYNAMICS**

SOUND ADVICE

Have students work toward vivid contrasts of dynamics.

263 **ARTICULATION AND DYNAMICS**

SOUND ADVICE

Remind students of the importance of a steady tempo as they exaggerate and contrast articulations and dynamics.

264 **ETUDE**

265 **CHORALE**

Randall D. Standridge (ASCAP)

266 **CHORALE**

Andrew Boysen, Jr.

267 **CONCERT A♭ MAJOR SCALE & CHORALE**

Chris M. Bernotas (ASCAP)

268 **CHORALE**

Ralph Ford (ASCAP)

269 **CHORALE**

Roland Barrett

Concert F Minor

270   PASSING THE TONIC

SOUND ADVICE

Have students hum exercises until they are comfortable with the idea of singing them.

271 BREATHING AND LONG TONES

SOUND ADVICE

Encourage students to draw full, sustained breaths through every beat of each rest.

▶ Snare Drum: This exercise incorporates the single ratamacue.

272   ## CONCERT F NATURAL MINOR SCALE

SOUND ADVICE

Remind students to completely depress keys or valves, and move slides quickly before making a sound.

▶ Snare Drum: Remind students to make the 9-stroke rolls even.

273 **CONCERT F HARMONIC AND MELODIC MINOR SCALES**

SOUND ADVICE

This exercise could also be performed with any number of students sustaining the first note as a drone to further develop intonation skills.

274 **SCALE PATTERN**

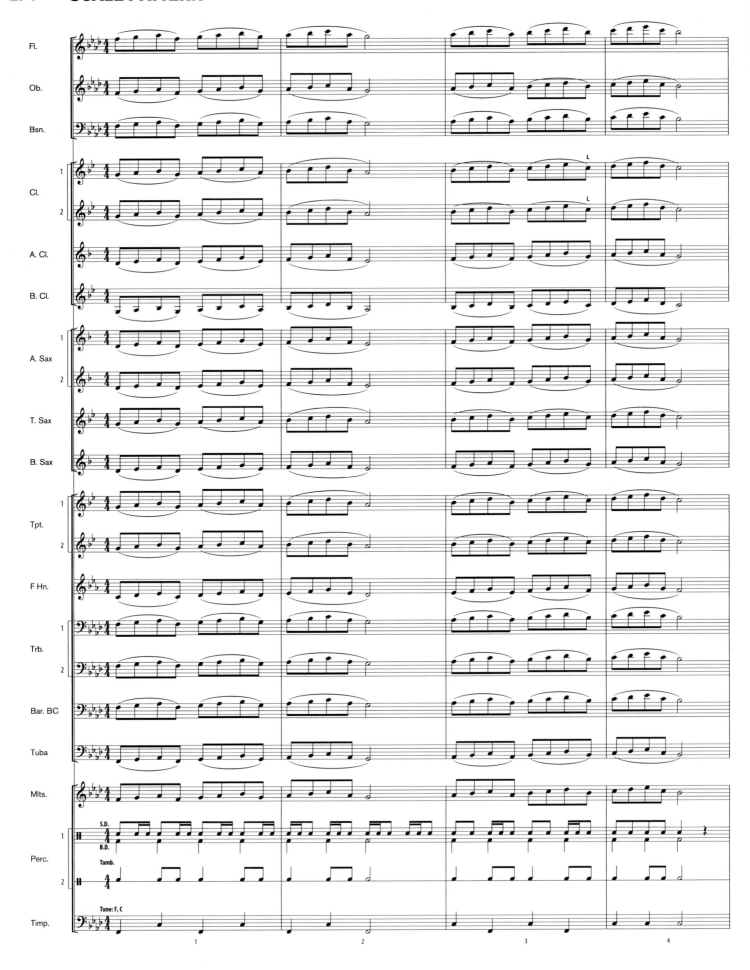

SOUND ADVICE
Remind students not to clip short the last note of slurred passages.

275 **CONCERT F CHROMATIC SCALE**

SOUND ADVICE
Clarinet, Alto Clarinet and Bass Clarinet: Remember to use chromatic alternate fingerings.

276 **FLEXIBILITY**

SOUND ADVICE

This exercise includes upward and downward leaps. This would be an excellent opportunity to discuss how embouchure, airstream and tongue position make this possible.

▶ Horn: The entire exercise can be played open on the F side. Be careful not to hit the (false) B♭ while slurring up or down.

277 **FLEXIBILITY**

SOUND ADVICE

Suggest that students push the airstream faster for upward leaps in pitch.

▶ Horn: The entire exercise can be played open on the F side. Be careful not to hit the (false) B♭ while slurring up or down. In measures, 4–8, be careful not to play the open E between the C and G. Keep good breath support, a firm embouchure, and change notes very quickly. Using the syllables "tah-ee" (low to high) or "tee-ah" (high to low) may help.

278 **ARPEGGIOS**

SOUND ADVICE

▶ Brass: Players should consider trying different syllables, such as "daw" or "taw," to help achieve lower notes, and "dee" or "tee" to help achieve higher notes.

279 **ARPEGGIOS**

SOUND ADVICE

Have students perform this exercise using a variety of articulations and dynamics.

280 **INTERVALS**

SOUND ADVICE
Have half of the students sing or hum this exercise, while the other half plays.

281 **INTERVALS**

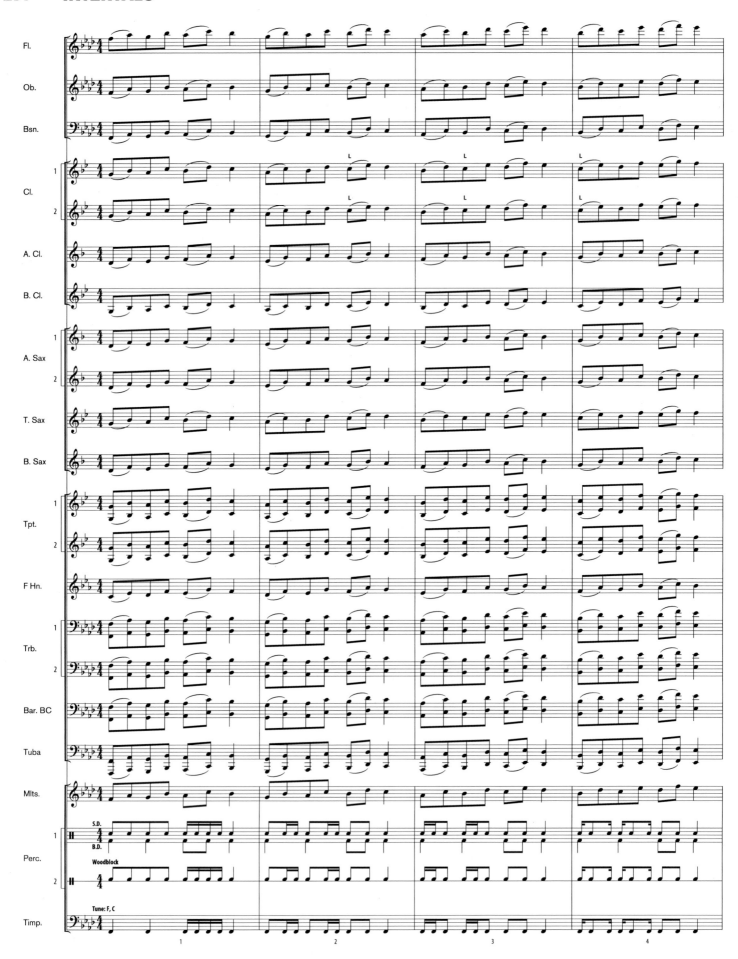

SOUND ADVICE

Have students master this exercise at a slow tempo and then gradually increase the speed to develop technical facility.

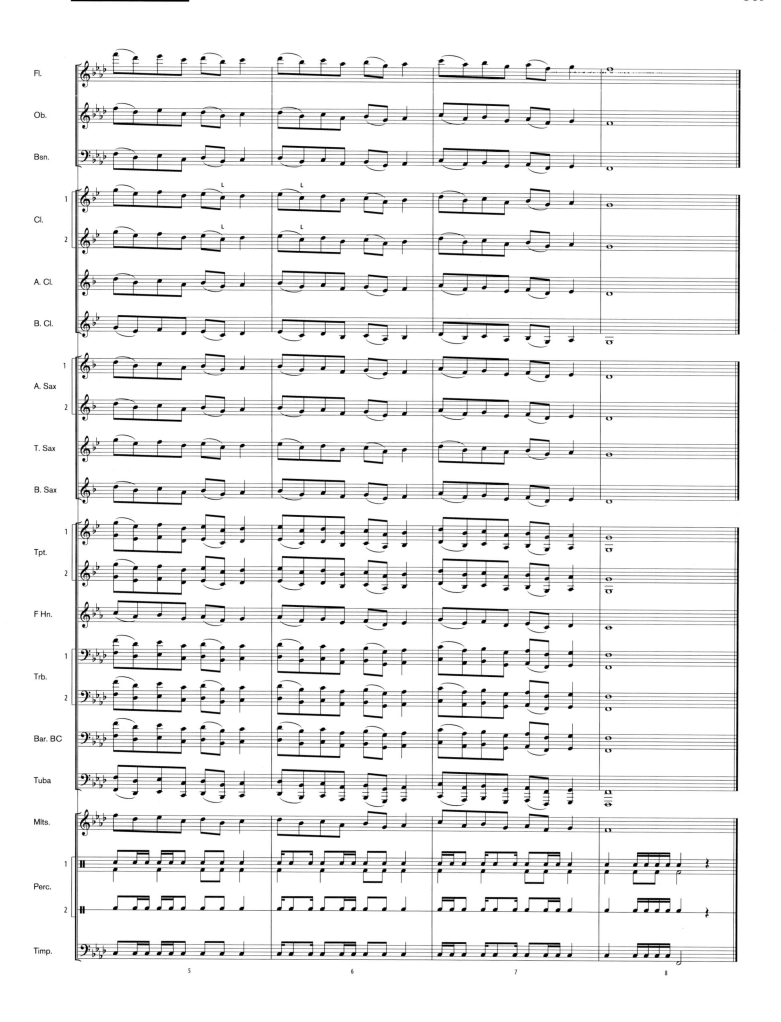

282 BALANCE AND INTONATION: DIATONIC HARMONY

SOUND ADVICE

Discuss with students the function of the harmonies in this exercise.

283 BALANCE AND INTONATION: FAMILY BALANCE

SOUND ADVICE

Discuss with students where best to release each note of this exercise.

284   **BALANCE AND INTONATION: LAYERED TUNING**

SOUND ADVICE
▶ Alto Saxophone: Discuss with students the pitch tendencies of notes in the upper register.

285   BALANCE AND INTONATION: MOVING CHORD TONES

SOUND ADVICE

This exercise could also be performed with any number of students sustaining the first note as a drone to further develop intonation skills.

286 EXPANDING INTERVALS: DOWNWARD IN TRIADS

SOUND ADVICE
Have the winds listen to the subdivision in the percussion to ensure accuracy of rhythm.

287 **EXPANDING INTERVALS: UPWARD IN TRIADS**

SOUND ADVICE

Remind students to sustain their dotted quarter rhythms for their full durations.

288 **RHYTHM**

SOUND ADVICE
Remind students that good tone quality requires excellent posture, hand position, embouchure and breathing.

289   **RHYTHM**

SOUND ADVICE

Have students perform this exercise using a variety of articulations and dynamics.

290 RHYTHM

SOUND ADVICE

This exercise can be played in 6 or in 2. With either choice, students should count all six beats to ensure accuracy.

291 **RHYTHMIC SUBDIVISION**

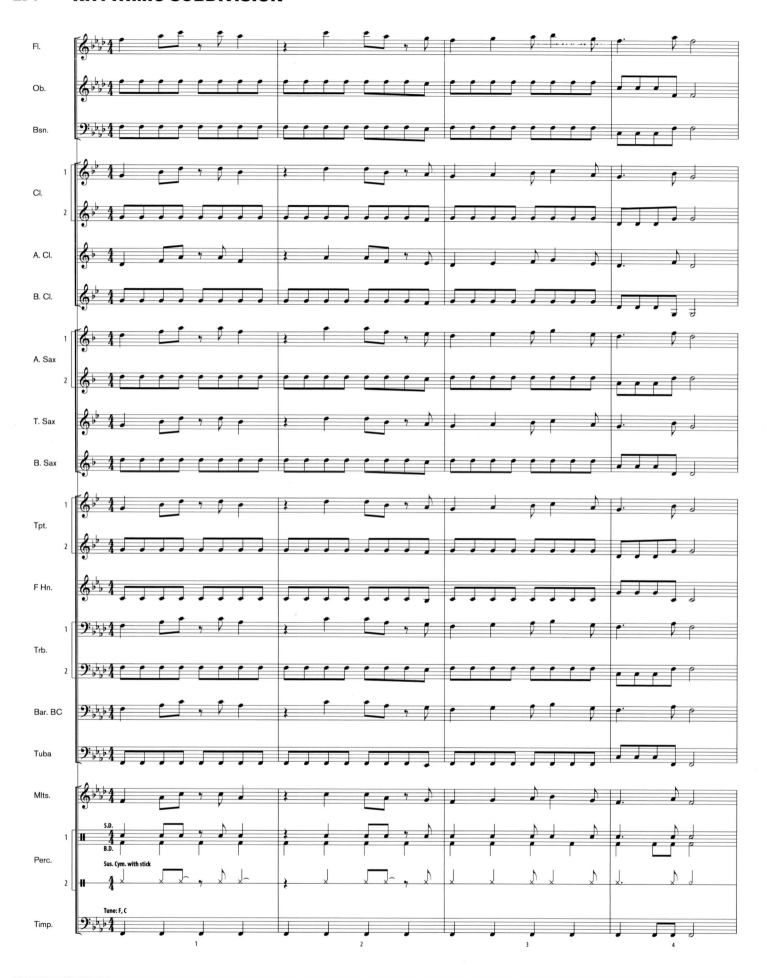

SOUND ADVICE

Have half the class conduct this exercise, while the other half claps or plays it.

292 **RHYTHMIC SUBDIVISION**

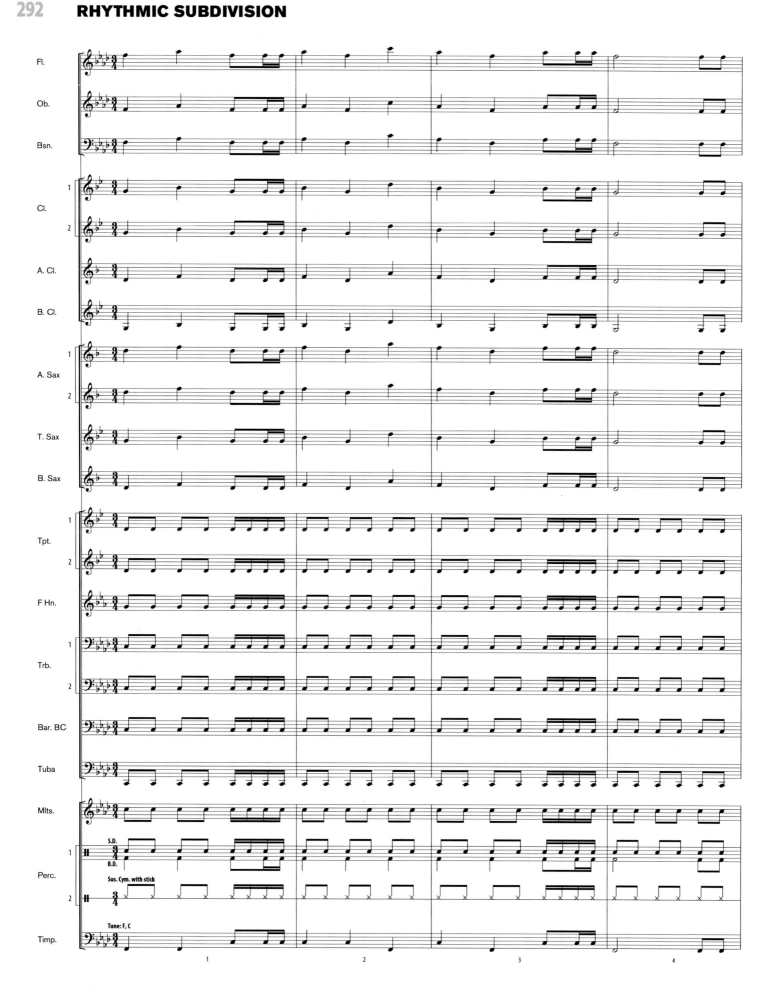

SOUND ADVICE

Remind students to think of tonguing as a way to clearly begin notes, as they push a continuous stream of air through the instrument.

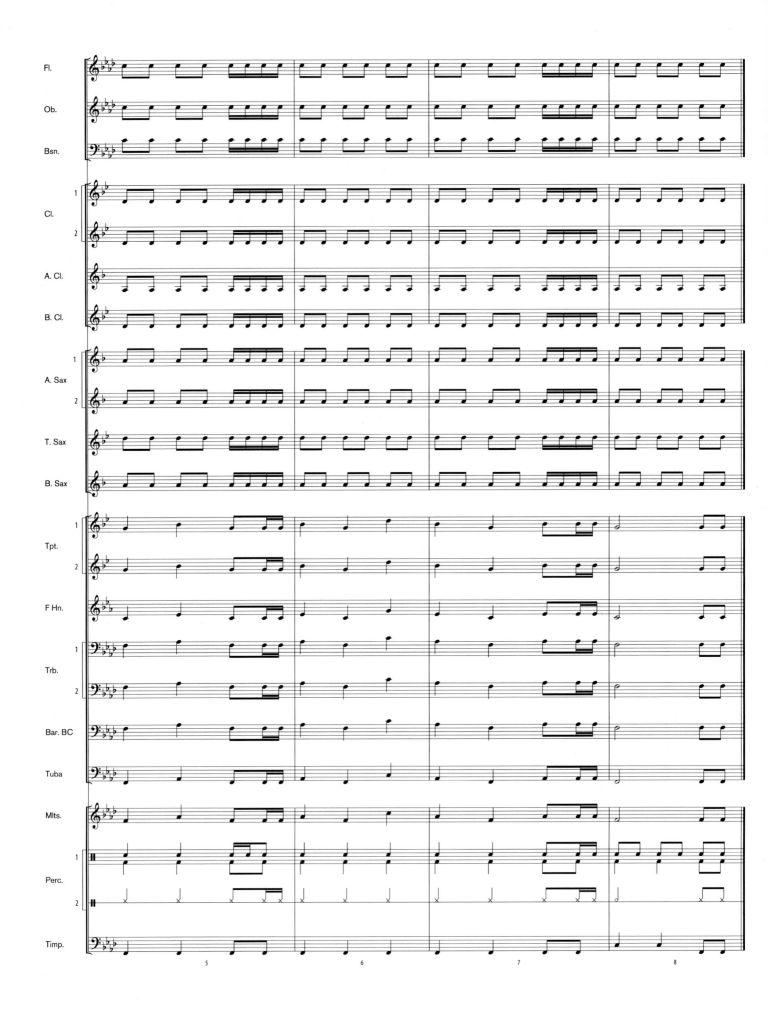

293

ARTICULATION AND DYNAMICS

SOUND ADVICE

Have students work toward vivid contrasts of articulation and dynamics.

294   ## ETUDE

295 **CHORALE**

Randall D. Standridge (ASCAP)

296 **CHORALE**

Roland Barrett

297 ## CONCERT F MINOR SCALE & CHORALE

Chris M. Bernotas (ASCAP)

298 **CHORALE**

Robert Sheldon

299 **CHORALE**

Ralph Ford (ASCAP)

Concert D♭ Major

300 **BREATHING AND LONG TONES**

SOUND ADVICE

Suggest to students a variety of approaches to breathing for this exercise.

301 CONCERT D♭ MAJOR SCALE

SOUND ADVICE

Encourage students to improvise melodies based on the notes of this scale.

302 **SCALE PATTERN**

SOUND ADVICE

Remind students to maintain a constant volume in the exercise as they ascend and descend through this scale.

303 **SCALE PATTERN**

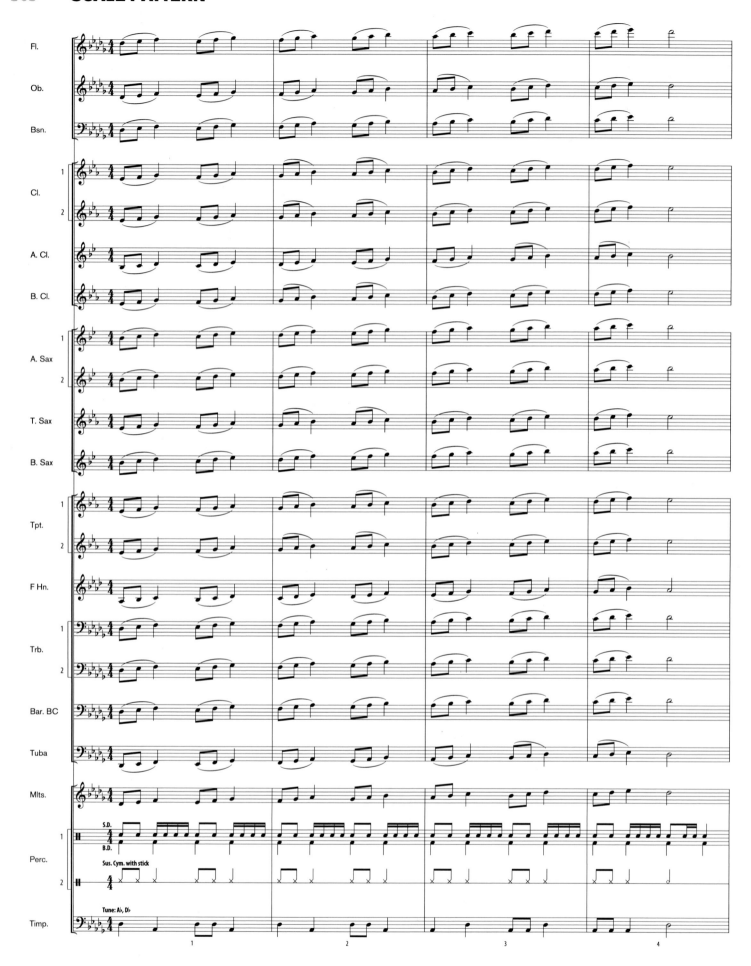

SOUND ADVICE

Discuss with students appropriate places to breathe in this exercise.

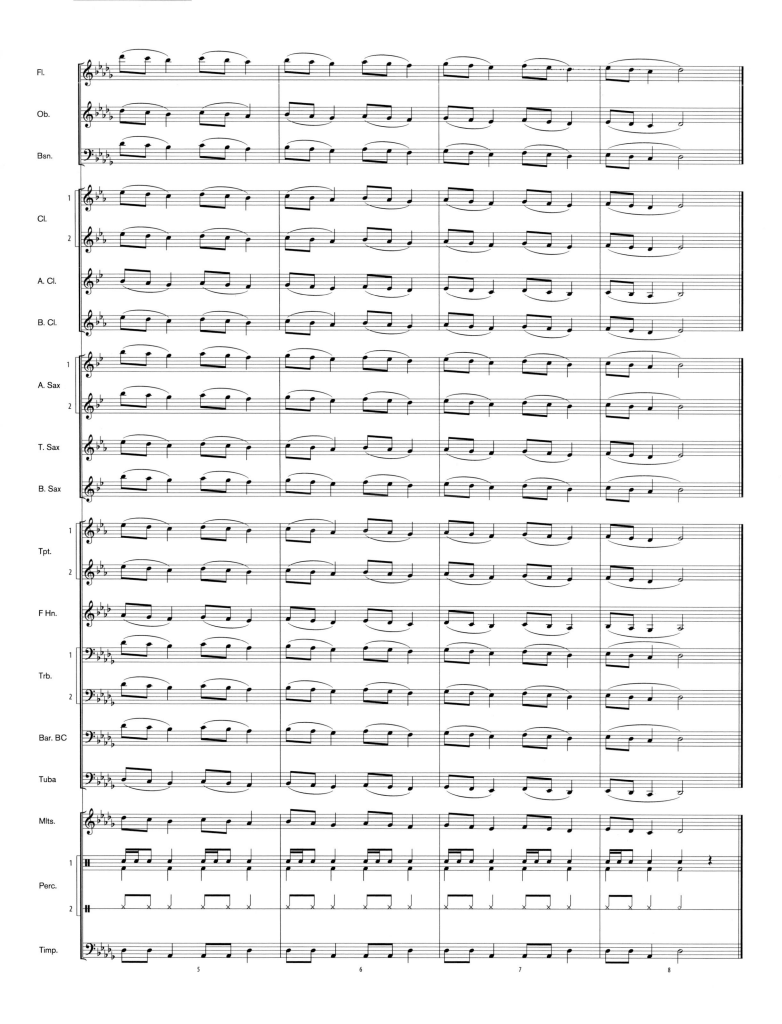

304 **SCALE PATTERN**

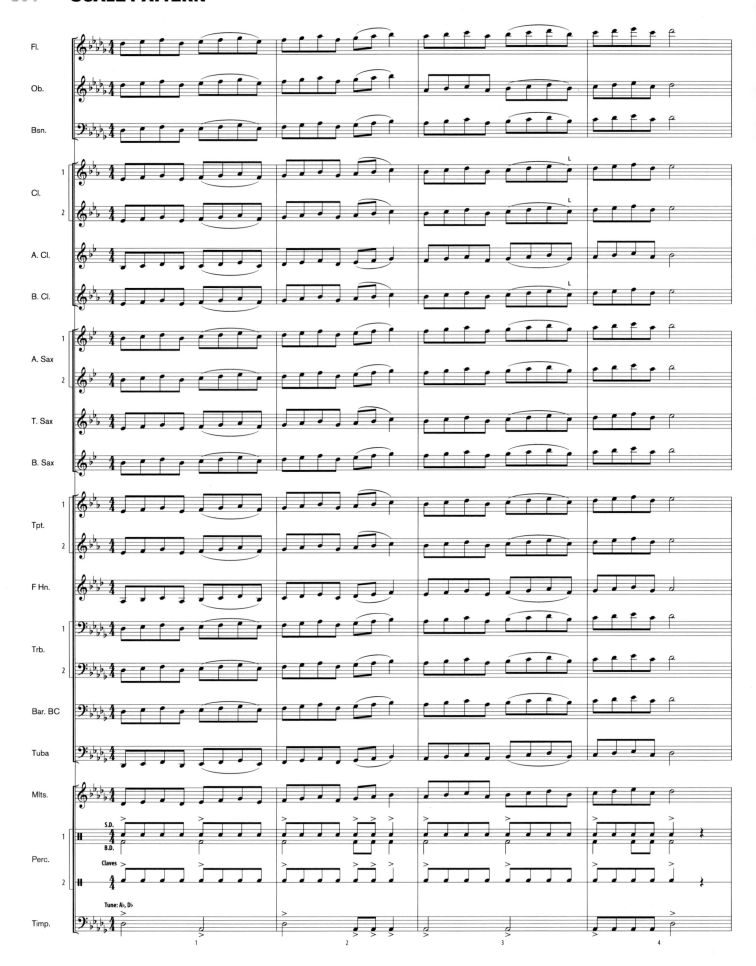

SOUND ADVICE

Encourage students to practice with a metronome.

▶ Brass: Remind students to use as little pressure against the lips as possible.

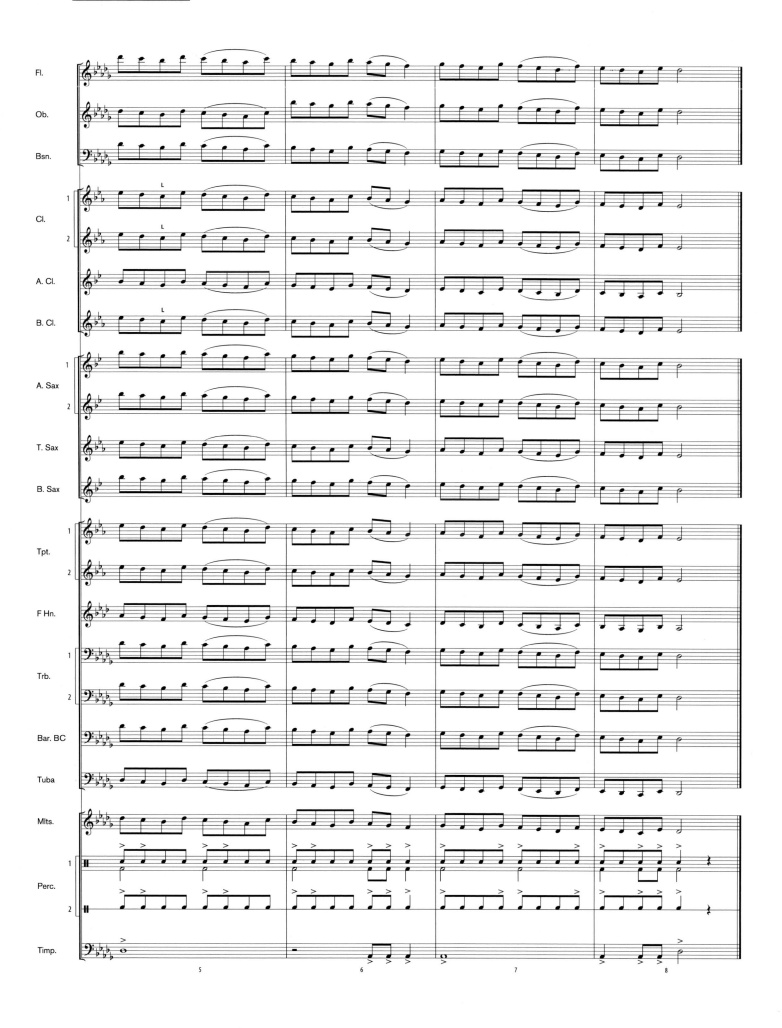

305   **FLEXIBILITY**

SOUND ADVICE

▶ Horn: Remind students that when playing a double horn, many teachers believe they should use F fingerings for second-line A♭ and lower, and B♭ fingerings for second-space A and higher.

306 ARPEGGIOS

SOUND ADVICE

Work to maintain a consistent tone quality while moving throughout the range of the instrument.

▶ Horn: Make certain students have their hands in the bell correctly. Also, to play in the lower range, it may help to use the syllable "taw," which will lower the jaw slightly.

307 **INTERVALS**

SOUND ADVICE

Remind students not to clip the note before they breathe.

308 **BALANCE AND INTONATION: FAMILY BALANCE**

SOUND ADVICE

Discuss with students where best to release each note of this exercise.

▶ Snare Drum: Discuss with students how some rhythms sound the same, even though they can be written differently.

309 **BALANCE AND INTONATION: LAYERED TUNING**

SOUND ADVICE

Encourage students to listen to each other as they perform this exercise to further develop ensemble skills.

310 EXPANDING INTERVALS: DOWNWARD AND UPWARD IN PARALLEL OCTAVES

SOUND ADVICE

Stress the importance of deep, full breaths to sustain long phrases.

Encourage independence by having small groups or soloists perform this exercise.

311 ARTICULATION AND DYNAMICS

SOUND ADVICE

Remind students to keep a steady tempo through every *crescendo* and *decrescendo*.

Remind students that *crescendos* and *decrescendos* must be performed in a gradual manner.

312 **ETUDE**

313 **ETUDE**

314 **CHORALE**

Andrew Boysen, Jr.

315 **CHORALE**

Todd Stalter

Concert B♭ Minor

316 **BREATHING AND LONG TONES**

SOUND ADVICE

Have half of the students sing or hum this exercise, while the other half plays.

317 **CONCERT B♭ NATURAL MINOR SCALE**

SOUND ADVICE

To help students develop improvisation skills, have them improvise using the pitches in this exercise

318

CONCERT B♭ HARMONIC AND MELODIC MINOR SCALES

SOUND ADVICE

Encourage students to compose short melodies based upon these scales.

319 **SCALE PATTERN**

SOUND ADVICE
Remind students of the importance of a steady tempo and accurate internal subdivision of the pulse.

320   SCALE PATTERN

SOUND ADVICE

This exercise could also be performed with any number of students sustaining the first note as a drone to further develop intonation skills.

321 FLEXIBILITY

SOUND ADVICE

▶ Brass: Remind students to play higher notes by keeping a firm embouchure as they increase the speed of the airstream.

322 **ARPEGGIOS**

SOUND ADVICE
Ask students to work for clearly-defined movement between pitches.

323   **INTERVALS**

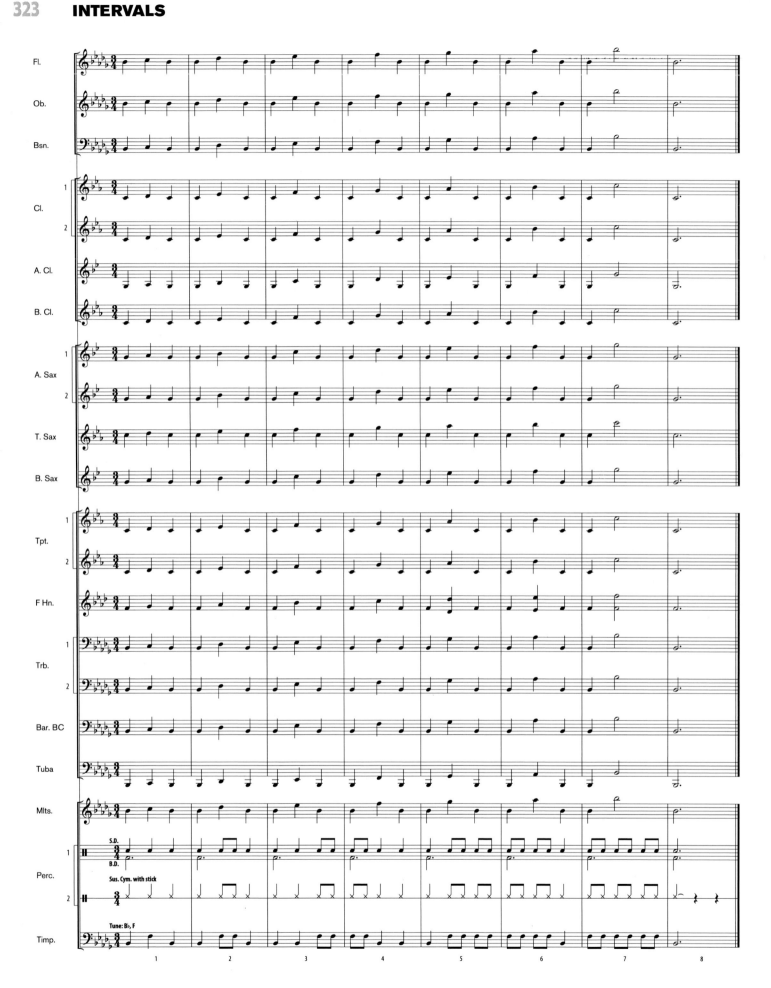

SOUND ADVICE

Have students work toward consistent tone quality as they ascend in this exercise.

324 **BALANCE AND INTONATION: LAYERED TUNING**

SOUND ADVICE

Encourage students to always warm up using long tones to help develop their tone quality.

325 BALANCE AND INTONATION: MOVING CHORD TONES

SOUND ADVICE

▶ Flute: Remind students that their instruments should be approximately parallel to the floor rather than pointed downward. They should also be reminded to never rest their right arms or elbows on the backs of their chairs.

326 EXPANDING INTERVALS: DOWNWARD IN TRIADS

SOUND ADVICE

▶ Trumpet, Baritone/Euphonium and Tuba: This would be a good time to remind students to use their fingertips to depress the valves to promote better technique.

327   **ARTICULATION AND DYNAMICS**

SOUND ADVICE

Remind students not to *diminuendo* during measure 4 to help provide a vivid contrast when moving to the *subito piano* in measure 5.

▶ Mallets: Use finger dampening for the notes marked with a staccato.

328 **ETUDE**

329 **ETUDE**

330 **CHORALE**

Michael Story (ASCAP)

331 **CHORALE**

Robert Sheldon

Concert C Major

332 **BREATHING AND LONG TONES**

SOUND ADVICE

▶ Woodwinds (except Flute): Encourage students to always have at least one extra reed available. Many teachers encourage students to have at least three reeds and rotate their use every day.

▶ Trumpet: Discuss with students when to use the third valve slide and its importance.

333 ## CONCERT C MAJOR SCALE

SOUND ADVICE

▶ Clarinet and Bass Clarinet: Suggest for students to use the left-hand B and right-hand C♯ throughout this exercise.

334 **SCALE PATTERN**

SOUND ADVICE

▶ Clarinet and Bass Clarinet: Suggest for students to use the left-hand B and right-hand C♯ throughout this exercise.

▶ Snare Drum: This exercise incorporates the triple paradiddle.

335 **SCALE PATTERN**

SOUND ADVICE

Challenge students to see how many notes they can play in one breath.

336 **FLEXIBILITY**

SOUND ADVICE

Remind students to pay as much attention to the releases of the notes as they do to the attacks.

▶ Trumpet: Discuss with students when to use the third valve slide and its importance.

337 ARPEGGIOS

SOUND ADVICE

Students must practice changing notes with deliberate, quick and smooth finger and hand movements.

338 **INTERVALS**

SOUND ADVICE

Have half the class conduct this exercise, while the other half performs it as written.

339 **INTERVALS**

SOUND ADVICE

▶ Clarinet and Bass Clarinet: Suggest for students to use the left-hand B and right-hand C♯ throughout this exercise.

340 **BALANCE AND INTONATION: FAMILY BALANCE**

SOUND ADVICE

Have students work toward melding their sound into that of the ensemble.

341   BALANCE AND INTONATION: LAYERED TUNING

SOUND ADVICE

Encourage students to stagger breathe as necessary.

342 EXPANDING INTERVALS: DOWNWARD IN PARALLEL FIFTHS

SOUND ADVICE

Remind students to keep their shoulders relaxed.

Guard against students puffing their cheeks.

343   ARTICULATION AND DYNAMICS

SOUND ADVICE

Discuss with students the difference between regular accents and marcato accents in this exercise

344 **ETUDE**

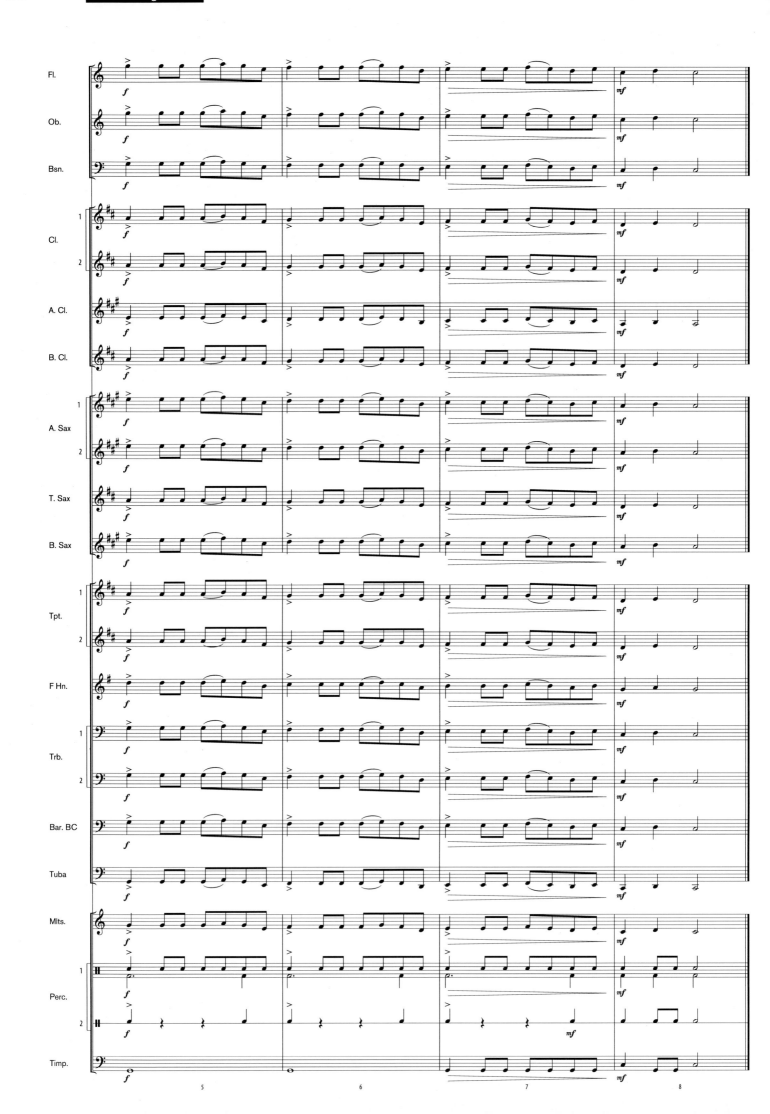

345 **ETUDE**

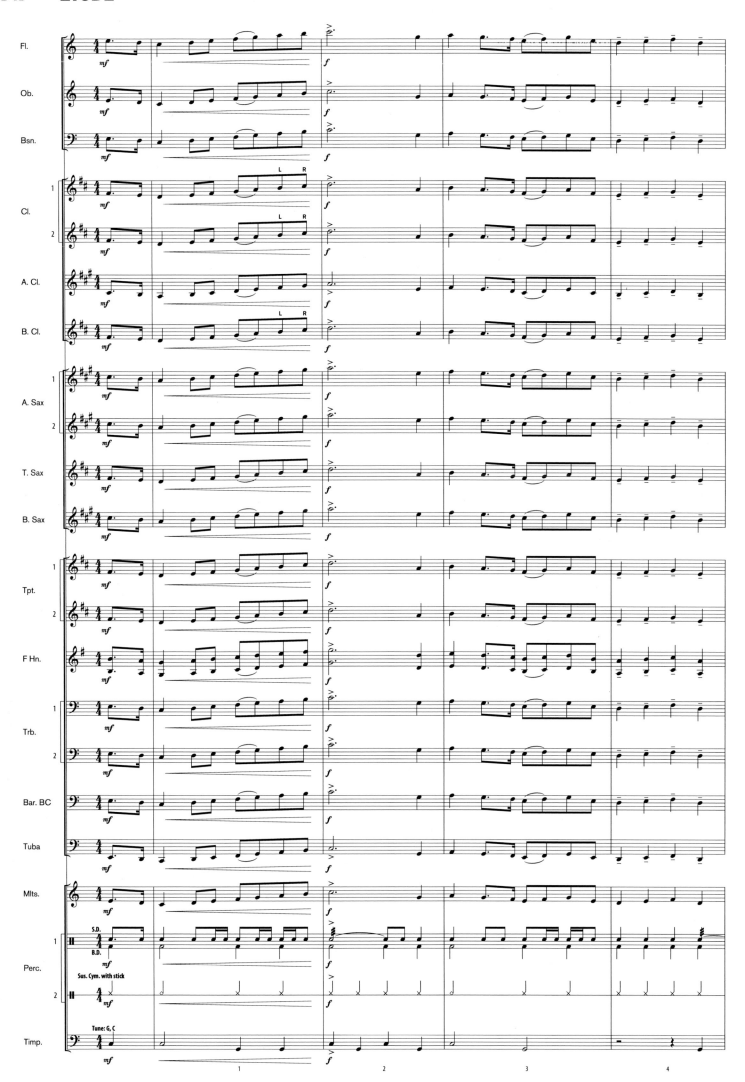

346 **CHORALE**

Ralph Ford (ASCAP)

347
CHORALE: LARGO FROM THE "NEW WORLD SYMPHONY"

Antonín Dvořák
Arranged by Michael Story (ASCAP)

Concert A Minor

348 **BREATHING AND LONG TONES**

SOUND ADVICE

For variety, have students "hiss" rather than play to help develop a steady and constant airstream.

349 **CONCERT A NATURAL MINOR SCALE**

SOUND ADVICE

Be insistent about students keeping their feet flat on the floor with their backs away from the chair.

350 ## CONCERT A HARMONIC AND MELODIC MINOR SCALES

SOUND ADVICE

▶ Alto Clarinet: Start this exercise with the left-hand F♯ and use the chromatic F♯ fingering as well.

▶ Brass: Remind students to use as little pressure against the lips as possible.

351 SCALE PATTERN

SOUND ADVICE
▶ Trumpet: Discuss with students when to use the third valve slide and its importance.

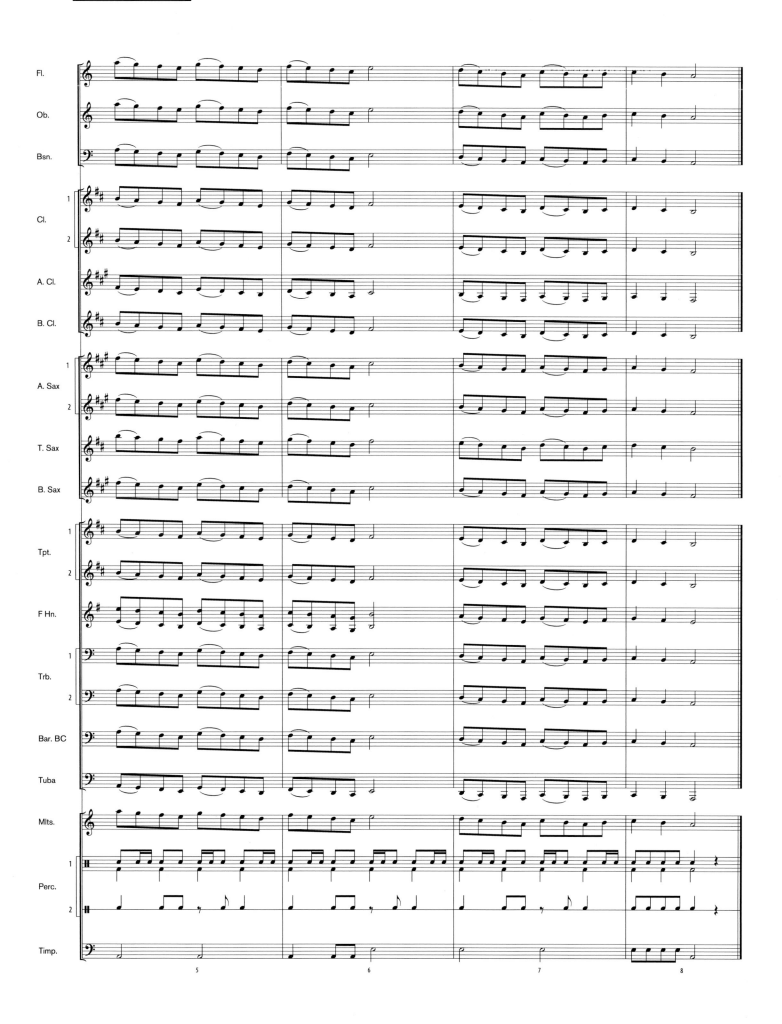

352 FLEXIBILITY

SOUND ADVICE

Discuss with students appropriate places to breathe in this exercise.

353 ARPEGGIOS

SOUND ADVICE

To encourage unified playing, discuss with students precisely how long and where they should breathe.

354 **INTERVALS**

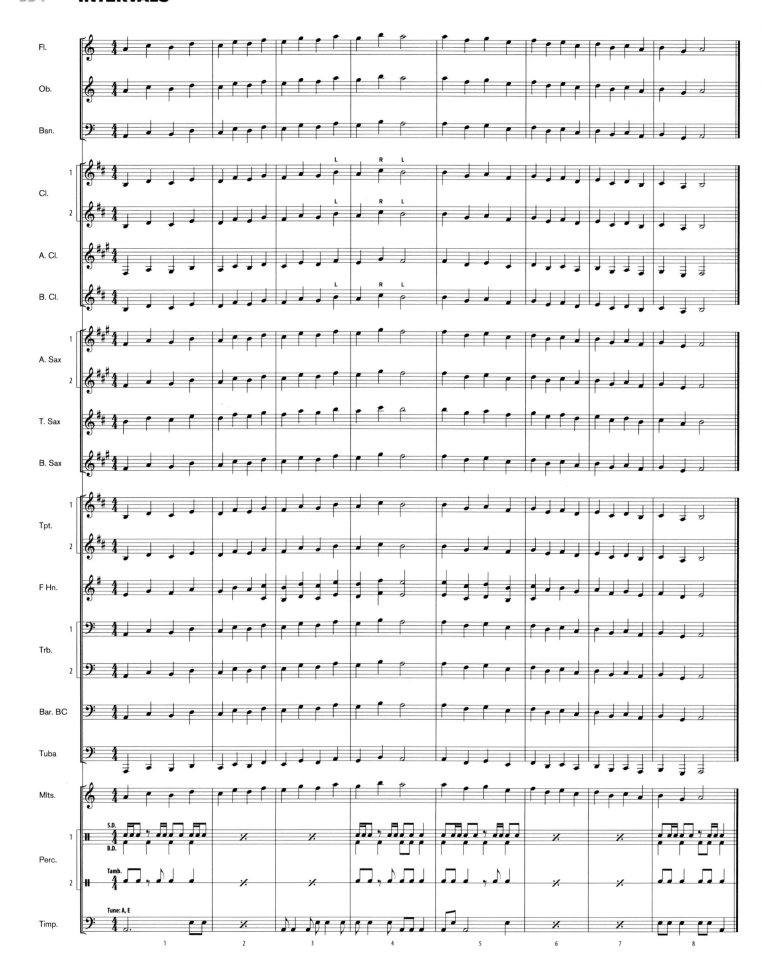

SOUND ADVICE

Have some brass students buzz this exercise on their mouthpiece, while other brass and/or woodwind students play it.

355 **INTERVALS**

SOUND ADVICE

Have half of the students sing or hum this exercise, while the other half plays.

356 **BALANCE AND INTONATION: DIATONIC HARMONY**

SOUND ADVICE

Brass and Woodwinds: Suggest that students not use lip gloss, lipstick or lip balm before playing their instruments.

357 BALANCE AND INTONATION: FAMILY BALANCE

SOUND ADVICE

Have half of the students sing or hum this exercise, while the other half plays.

358 **EXPANDING INTERVALS: DOWNWARD IN TRIADS**

SOUND ADVICE

Remind students not to clip short the last note of slurred passages.

359 **ARTICULATION AND DYNAMICS**

SOUND ADVICE

Encourage students to make their crescendos and decrescendos even and gradual.

360 **ETUDE**

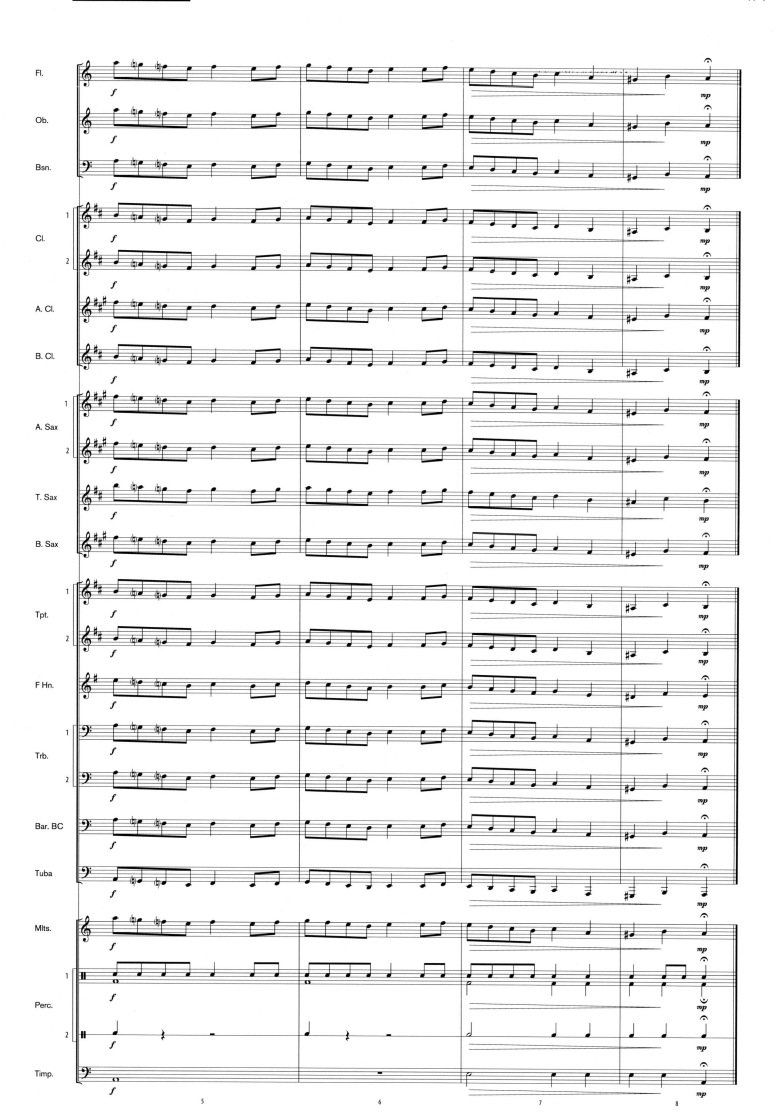

361   ETUDE

362 **CHORALE**

Todd Stalter

363 **CHORALE**

Roland Barrett

Concert G Major

364 **CONCERT G MAJOR SCALE**

SOUND ADVICE

▶ Snare Drum: This exercise incorporates the triple paradiddle.

365 BALANCE AND INTONATION: FAMILY BALANCE

SOUND ADVICE

Discuss with students the concept of family balance and how it relates to good ensemble balance.

366 **ETUDE**

367 **CHORALE**

Michael Story (ASCAP)

Concert E Minor

368

CONCERT E NATURAL MINOR SCALE

SOUND ADVICE

Remind students to completely depress keys or valves, and move slides quickly before making a sound.

369

CONCERT E HARMONIC AND MELODIC MINOR SCALES

SOUND ADVICE

Have students work toward consistent tone quality as they ascend and descend through these scales.

370 BALANCE AND INTONATION: LAYERED TUNING

SOUND ADVICE

Encourage students to be active listeners during rests to promote good ensemble playing.

371 ETUDE

CHORALE

Chris M. Bernotas (ASCAP)

Advancing Rhythm and Meter

373 $\frac{6}{8}$ **METER**

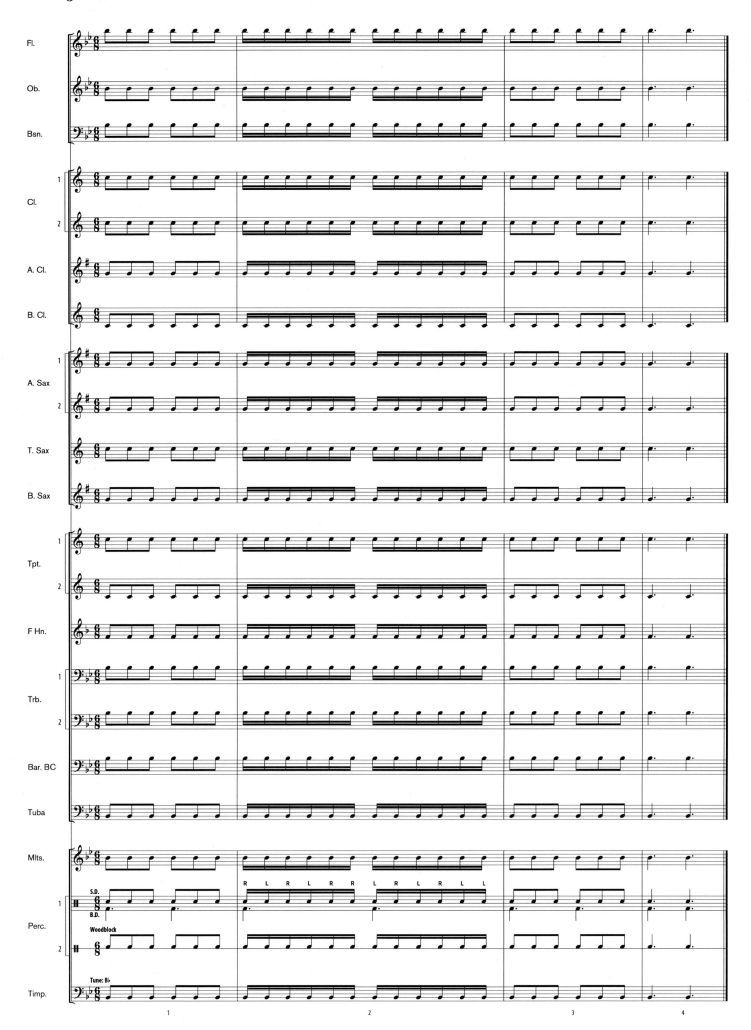

374 $\frac{6}{8}$ **METER**

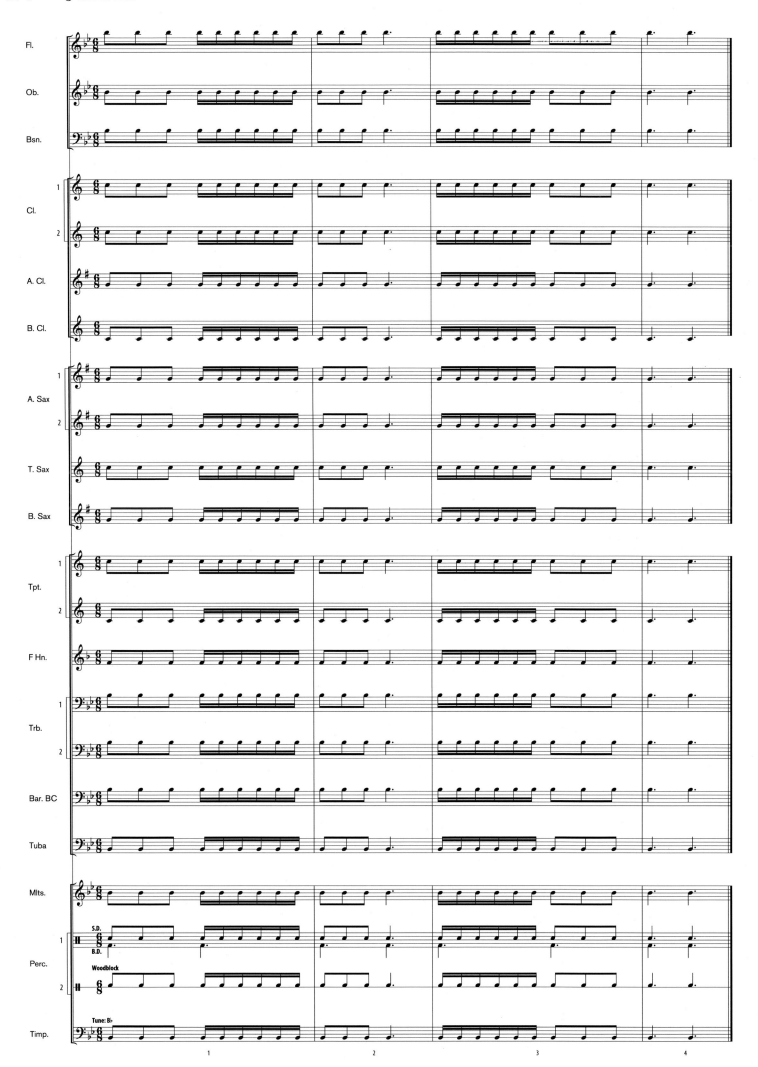

375 ⁶⁄₈ **METER**

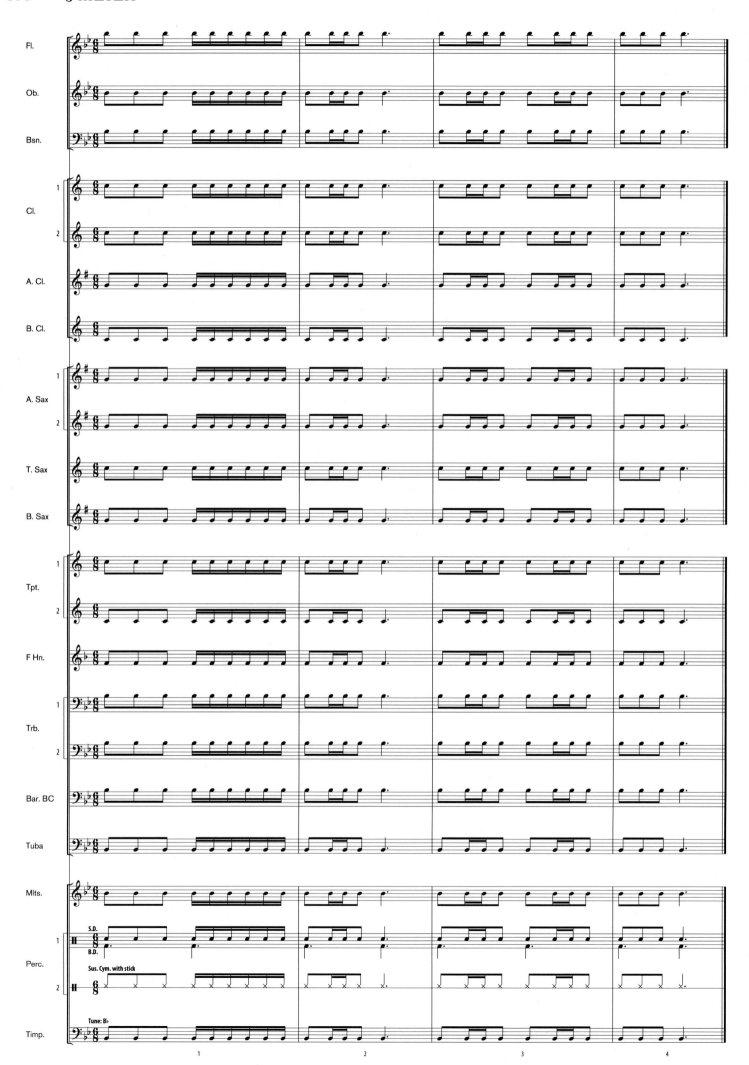

376 ⁶/₈ **METER**

377 $\frac{6}{8}$ **METER**

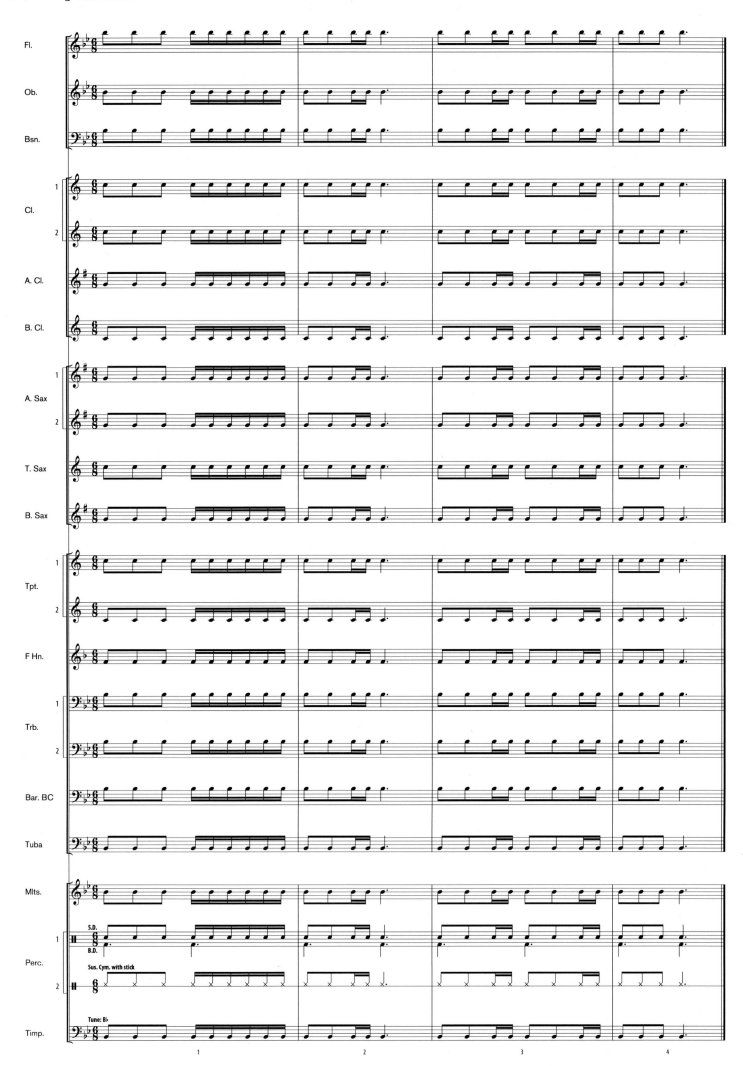

378 $\frac{6}{8}$ **METER**

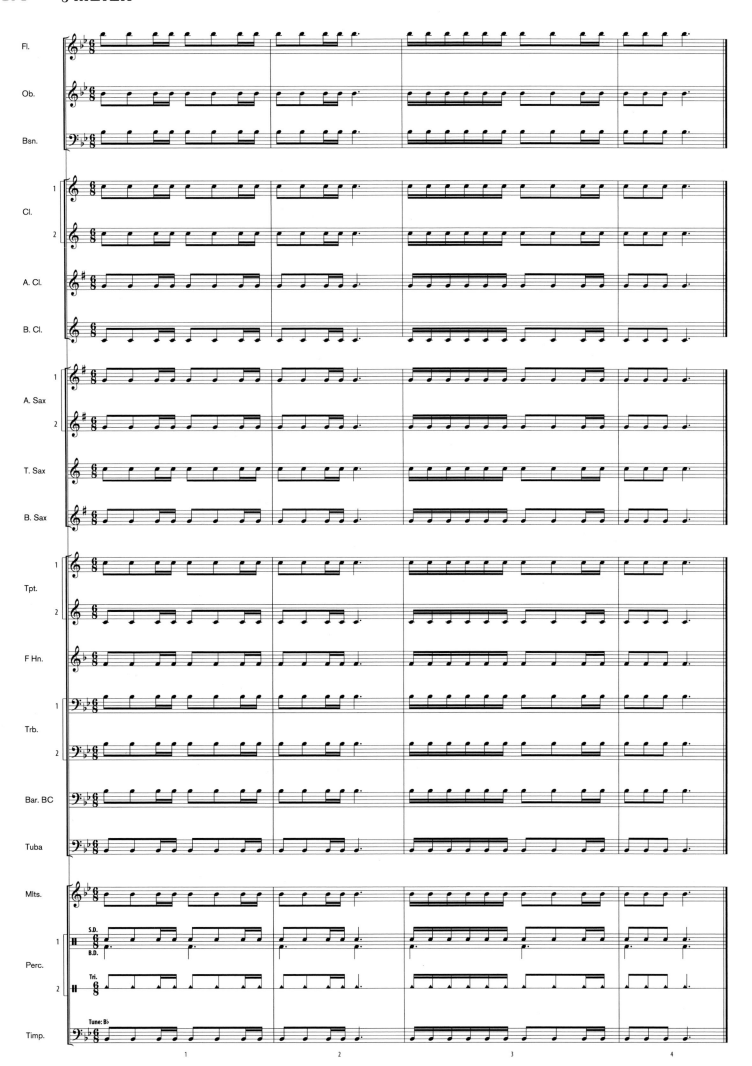

379 ♪⁶⁄₈ **METER**

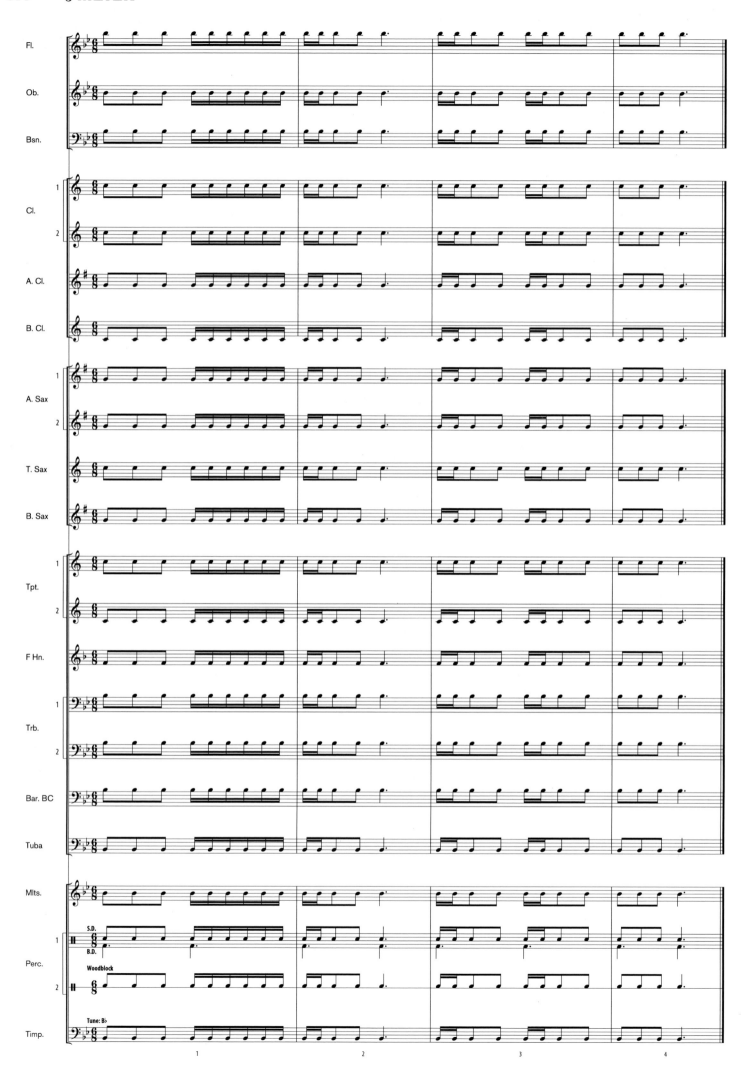

380 $\frac{6}{8}$ **METER**

381 $\frac{6}{8}$ METER

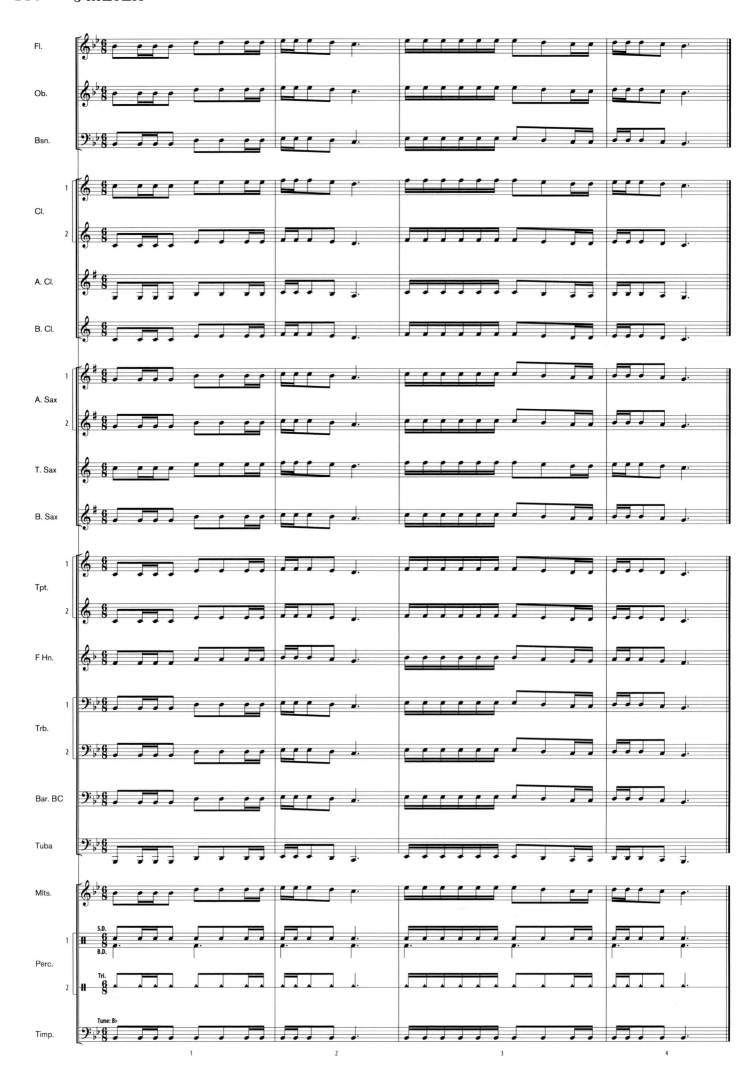

382 $\frac{6}{8}$ **METER**

383 $\frac{6}{8}$ **METER**

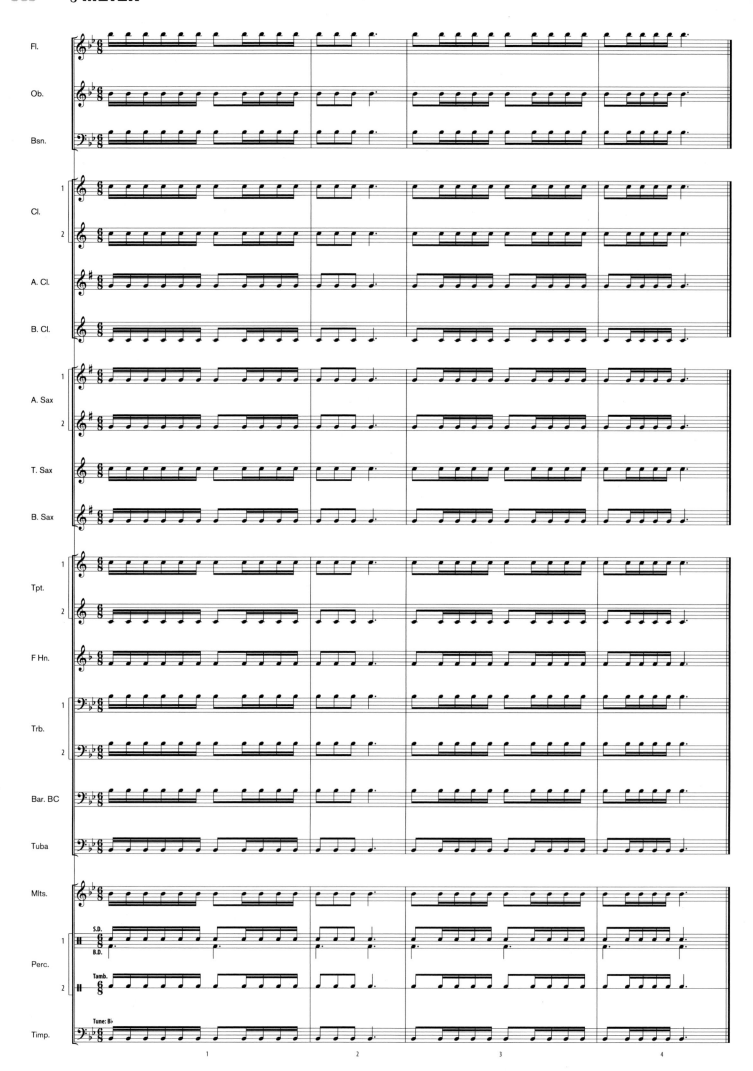

384 $\frac{6}{8}$ **METER**

385 $\frac{6}{8}$ **METER**

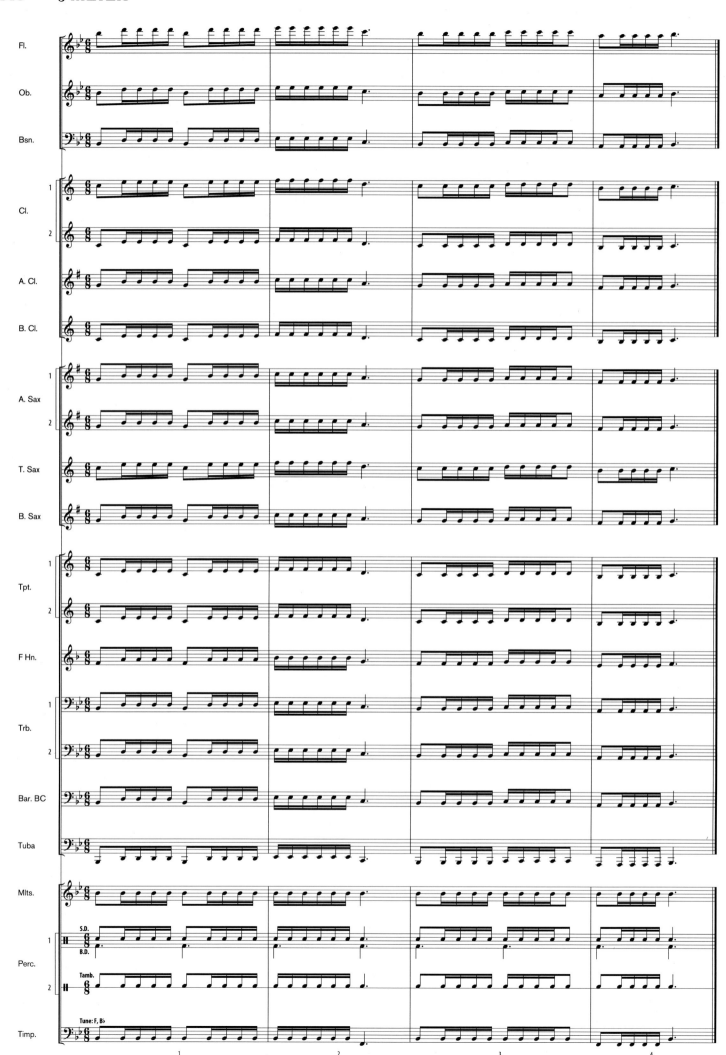

386 $\frac{6}{8}$ **METER**

387 $\frac{6}{8}$ **METER**

388 ⁶₈ **METER**

389    $\frac{6}{8}$ **METER**

390   **⁶⁄₈ METER**

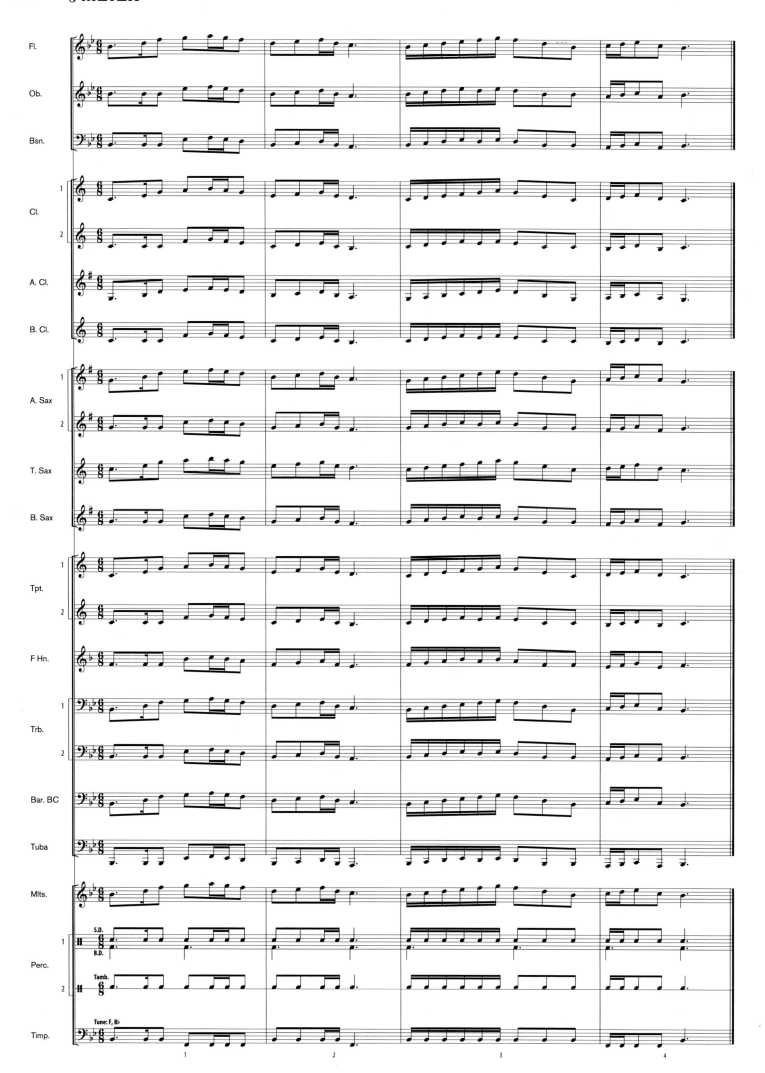

391 **CHANGING METERS: 4/4 AND 6/8**

392 ## CHANGING METERS: $\frac{3}{4}$ AND $\frac{6}{8}$

393 **TRIPLETS**

394 **TRIPLETS**

395   **TRIPLETS**

396 **TRIPLETS**

397   **TRIPLETS**

398 **TRIPLETS**

399 **TRIPLETS**

400 **TRIPLETS**

401 **TRIPLETS**

402 **TRIPLETS**

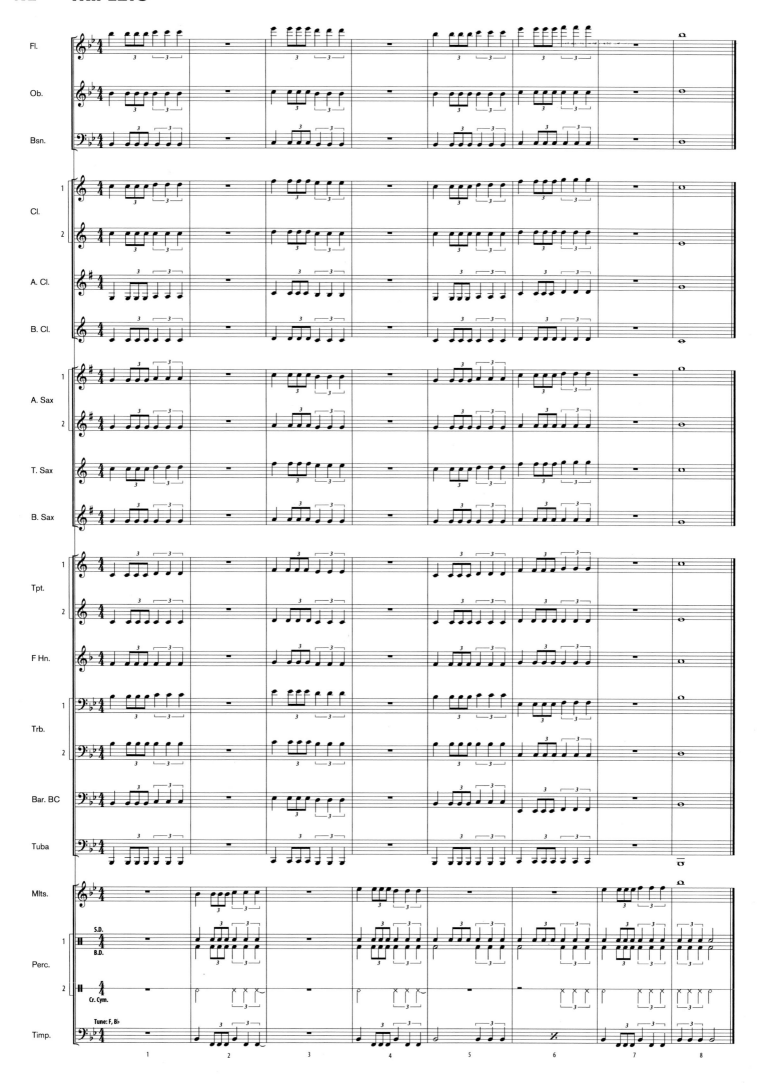

403 $\frac{3}{8}$ **METER**

404 $\frac{3}{8}$ **METER**

405　⁹⁄₈ **METER**

406   **⁹⁄₈ METER**

407 ¹²⁄₈ **METER**

408 **12/8 METER**

409 **⅝ METER**

410 **⅝ METER**

411 $\frac{7}{8}$ **METER**

(2+2+3)

412 $\frac{7}{8}$ **METER**

Flute Fingering Chart

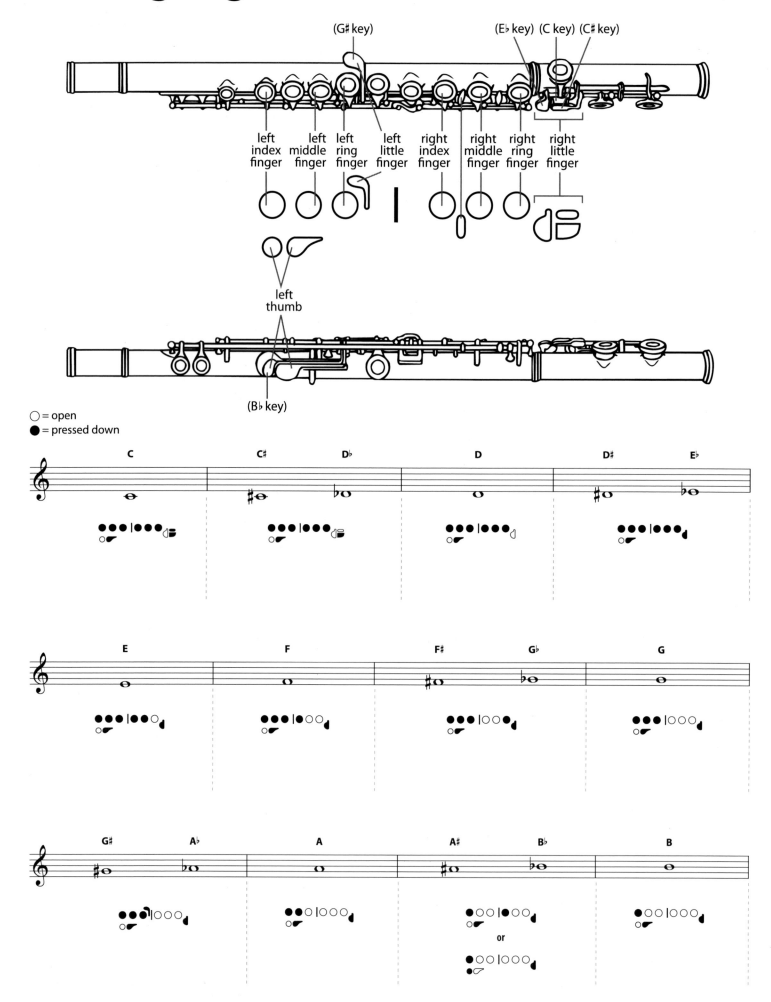

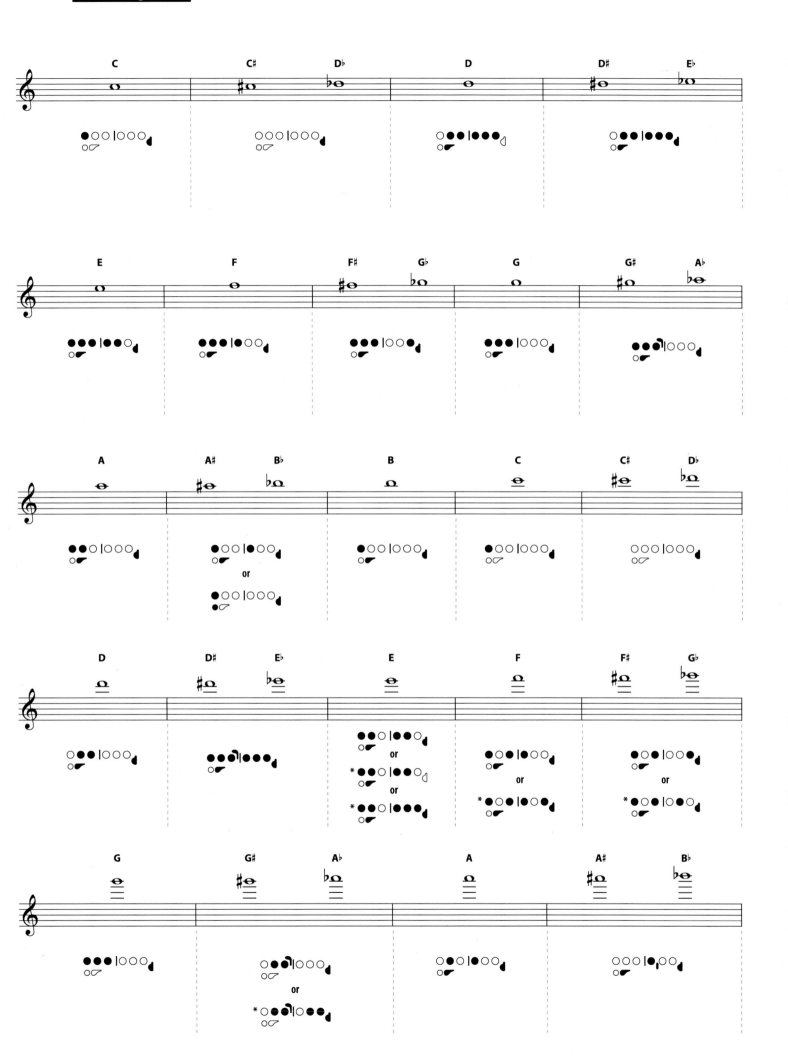

*This fingering may help stabilize pitch.

Oboe Fingering Chart

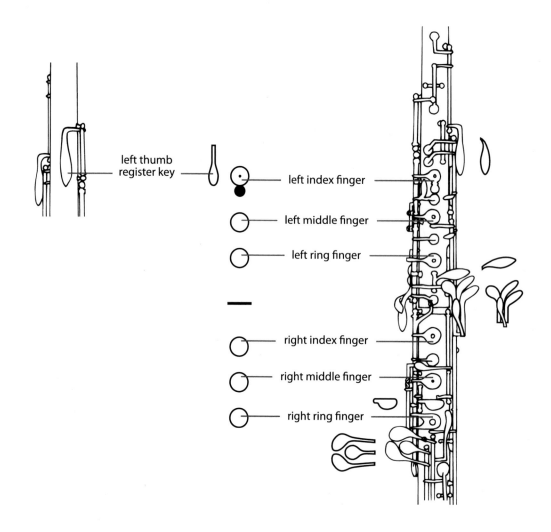

○ = open
● = pressed down

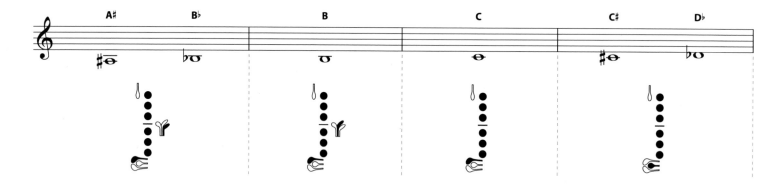

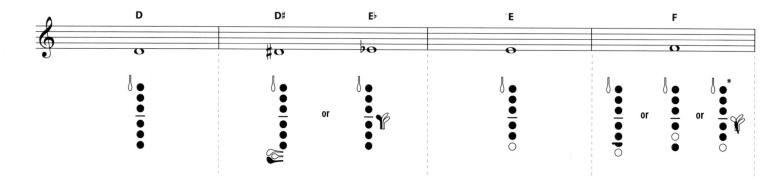

*For instruments that have this key.

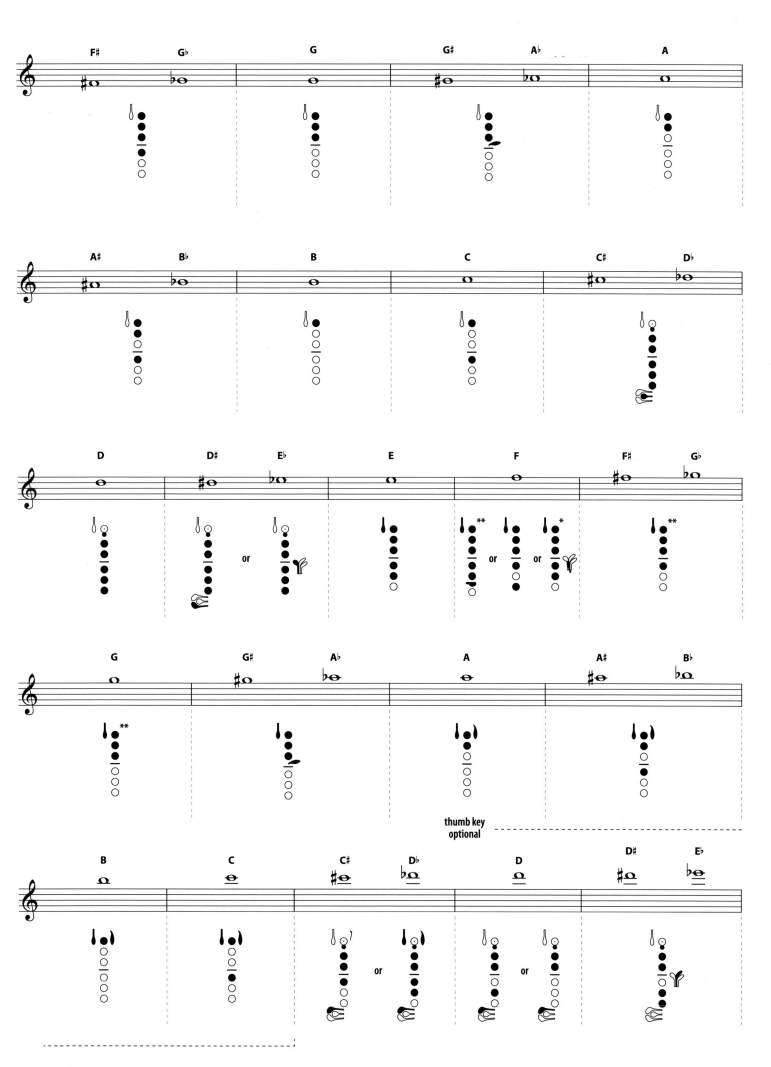

**The low B key can be added to help stabilize the pitch.

Bassoon Fingering Chart

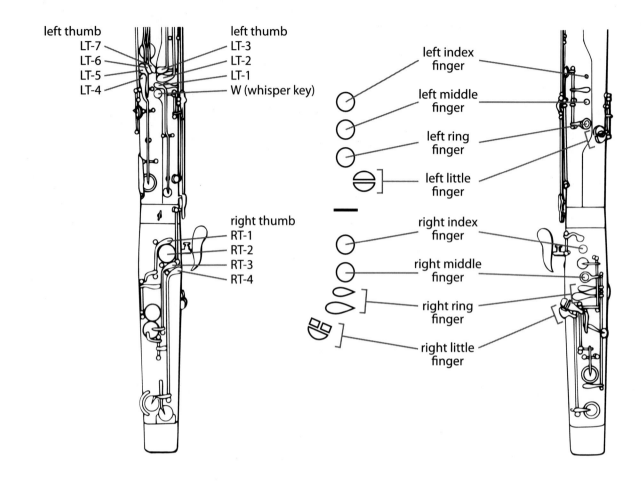

○ = open
● = pressed down
◒ = half hole covered
LT = left thumb
RT = right thumb

Bassoon players use a technique called flicking, not on any other instrument. This involves the momentary pressing (or "flicking") of the high A, C, or D keys by the left hand thumb at the beginning of certain notes in the middle octave in order to help achieve a better start to the note. Any note that is not responsive or cracks between octaves may benefit from using this technique.

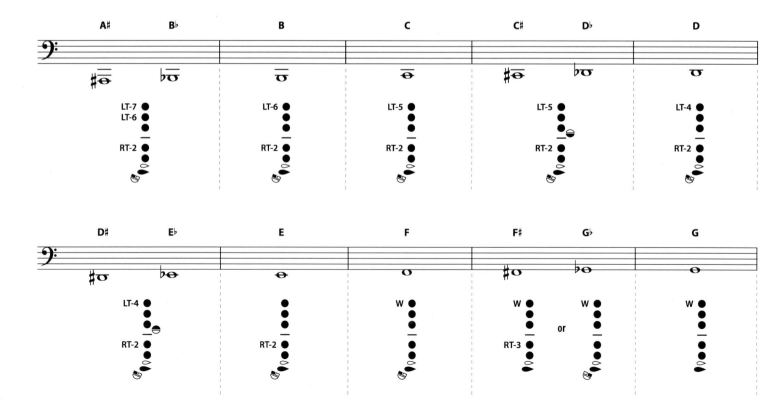

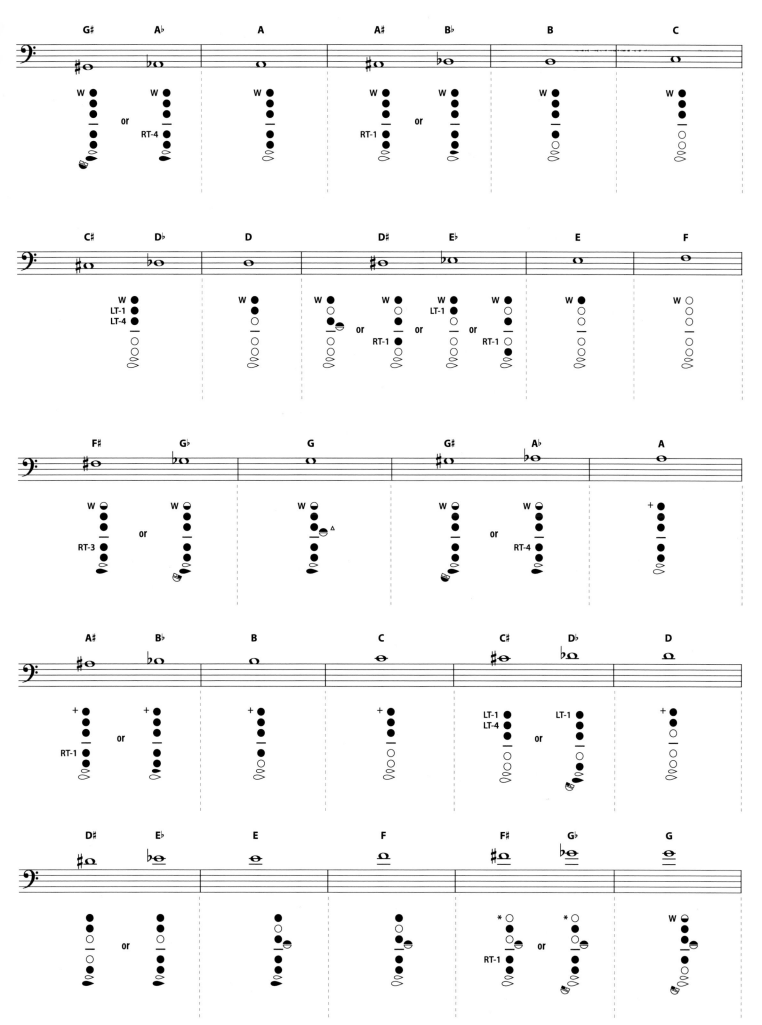

*On some bassoons, high F#/G♭ can be played more in tune by adding the left-hand 3rd (ring) finger to one of the standard fingerings.
+The stability of this note can be improved by touching or "flicking" LT-2 or LT-3 at the beginning of the note.
△Either left pinky can be used depending upon the intonation of the instrument.

Clarinet Fingering Chart

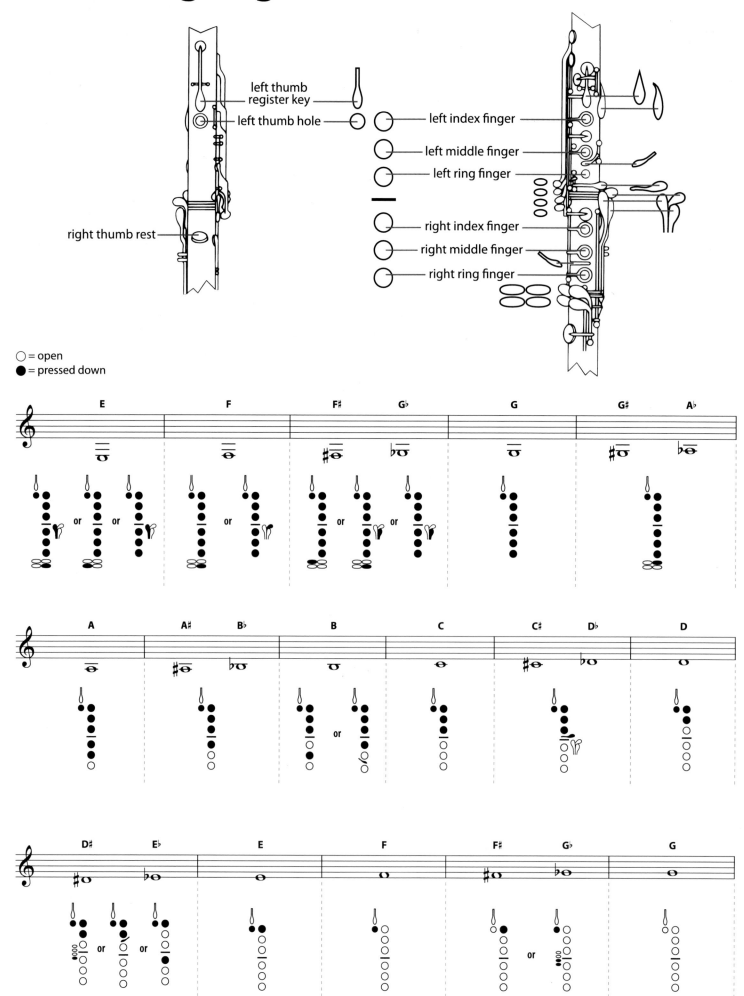

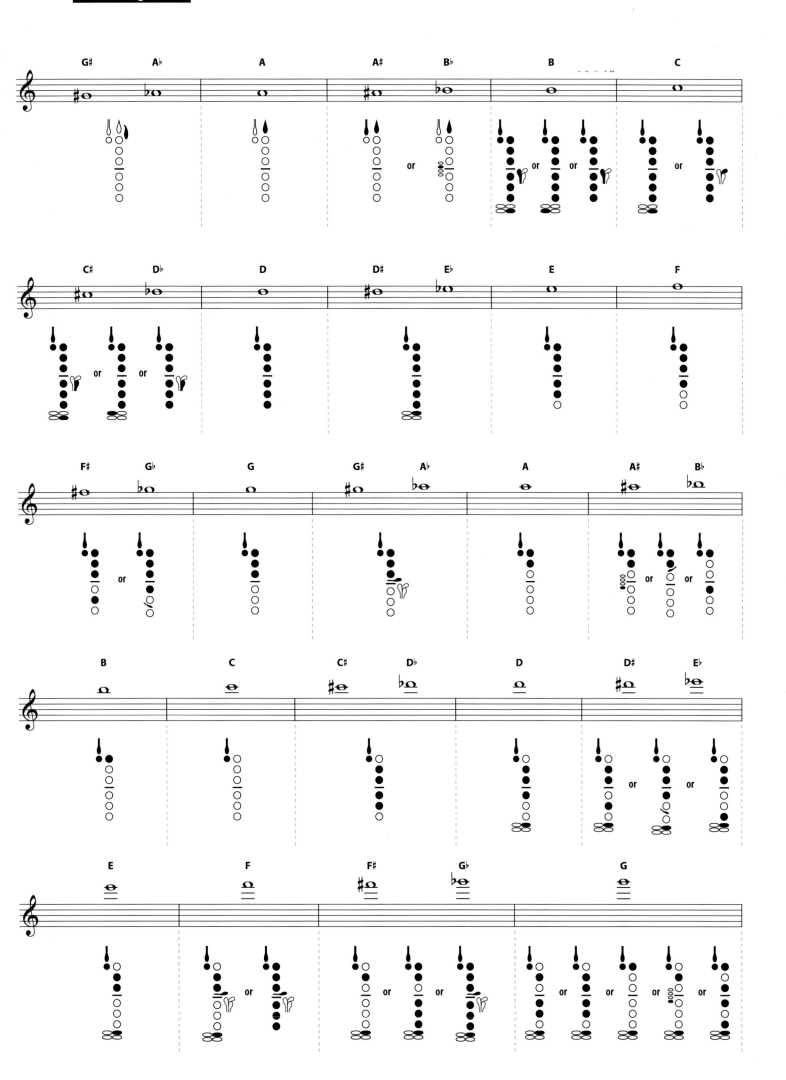

Alto Clarinet Fingering Chart

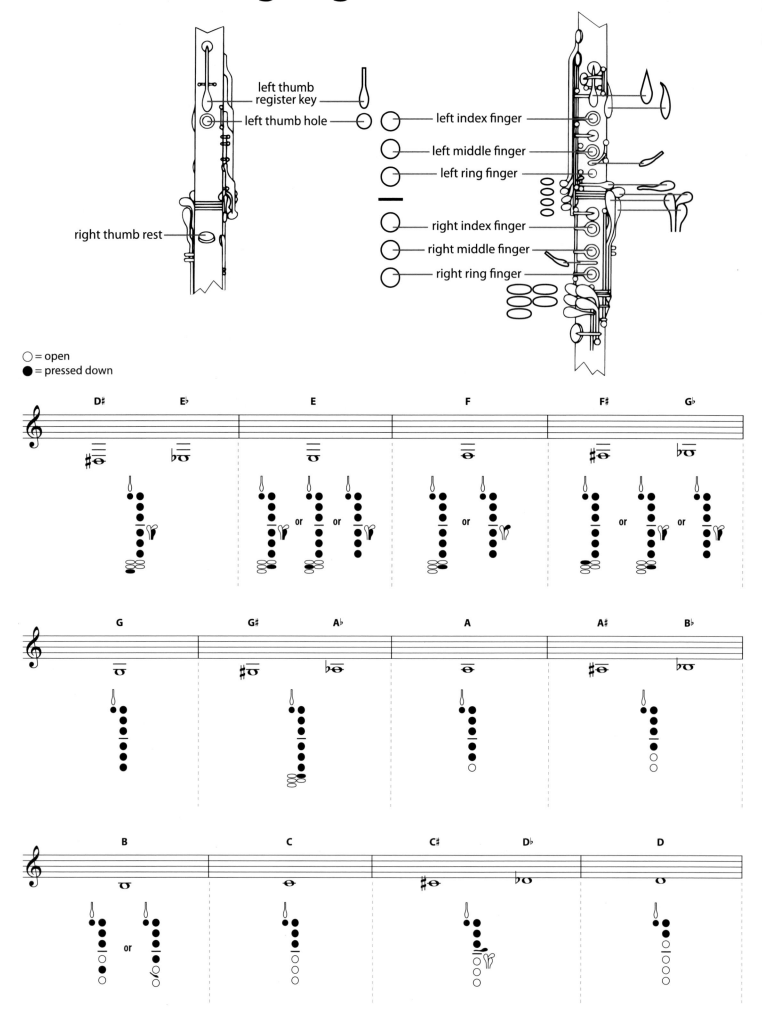

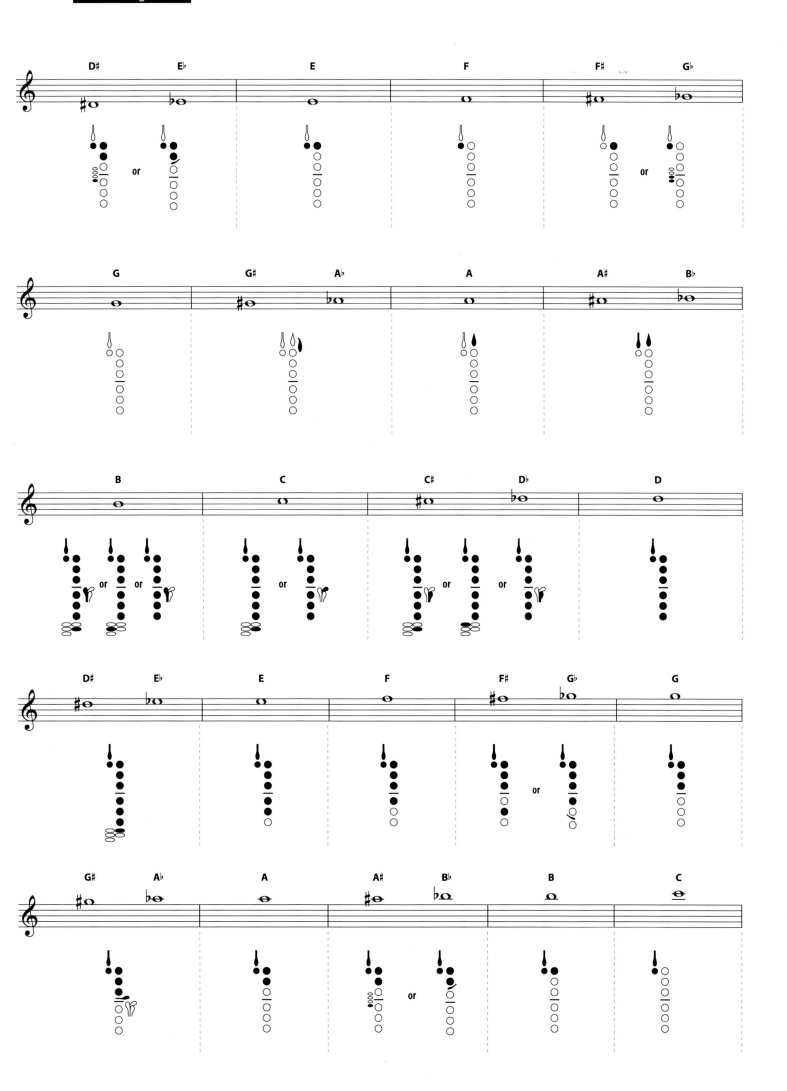

Bass Clarinet Fingering Chart

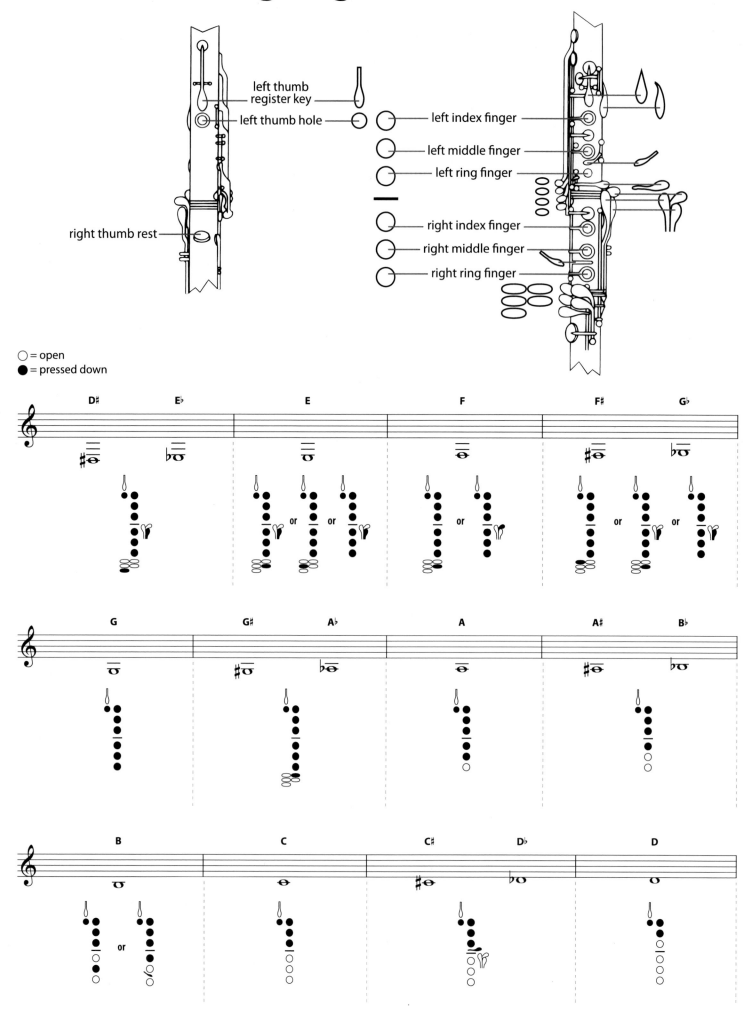

Alto Saxophone Fingering Chart

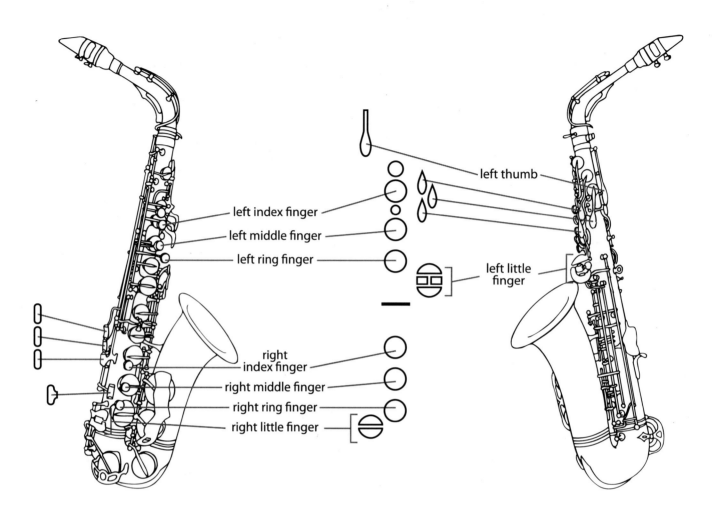

○ = open
● = pressed down

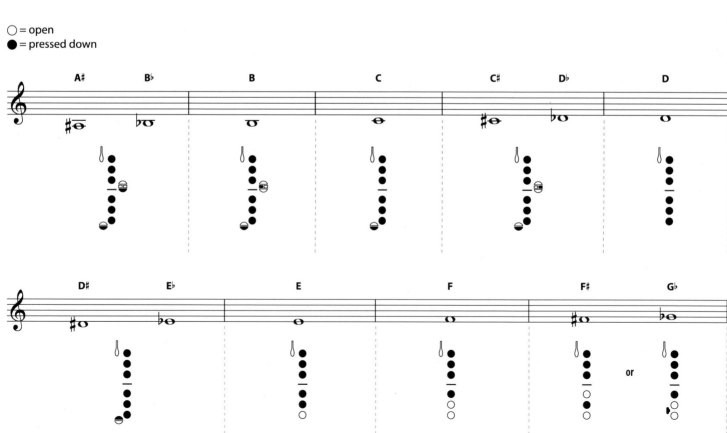

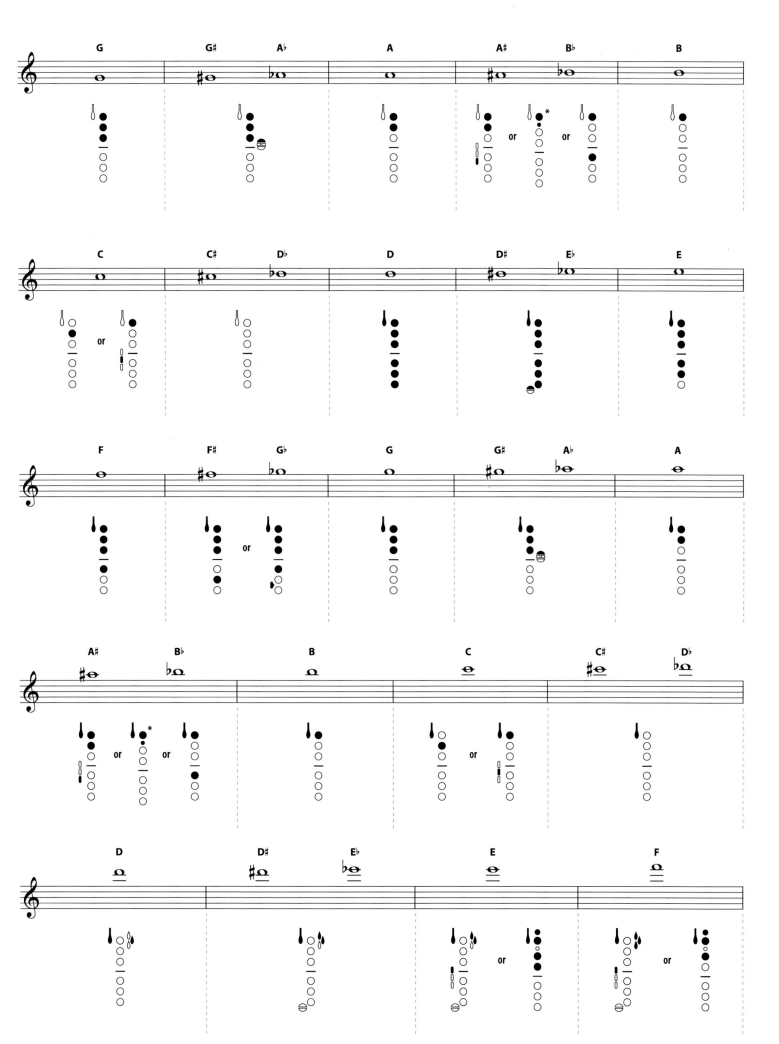

*The bis key is used for this fingering. This fingering should not be used in a chromatic scale.

Tenor Saxophone Fingering Chart

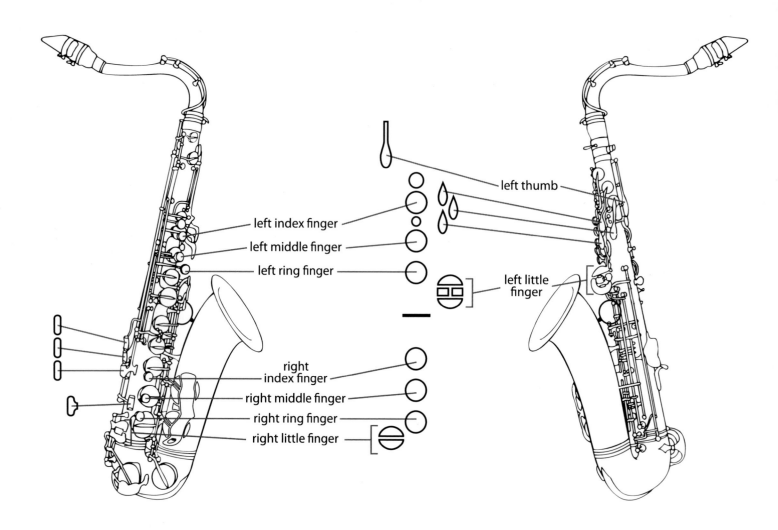

○ = open
● = pressed down

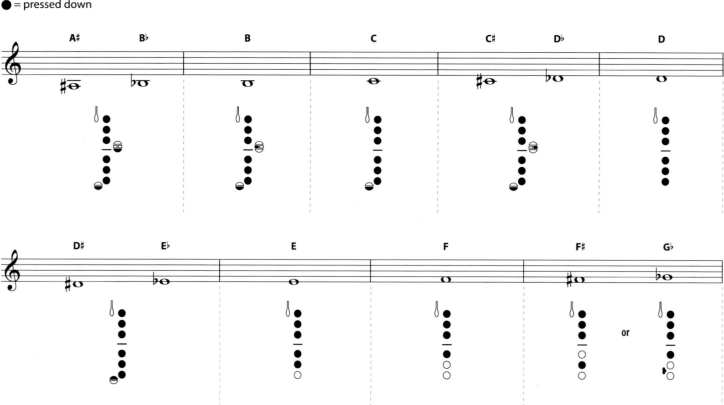

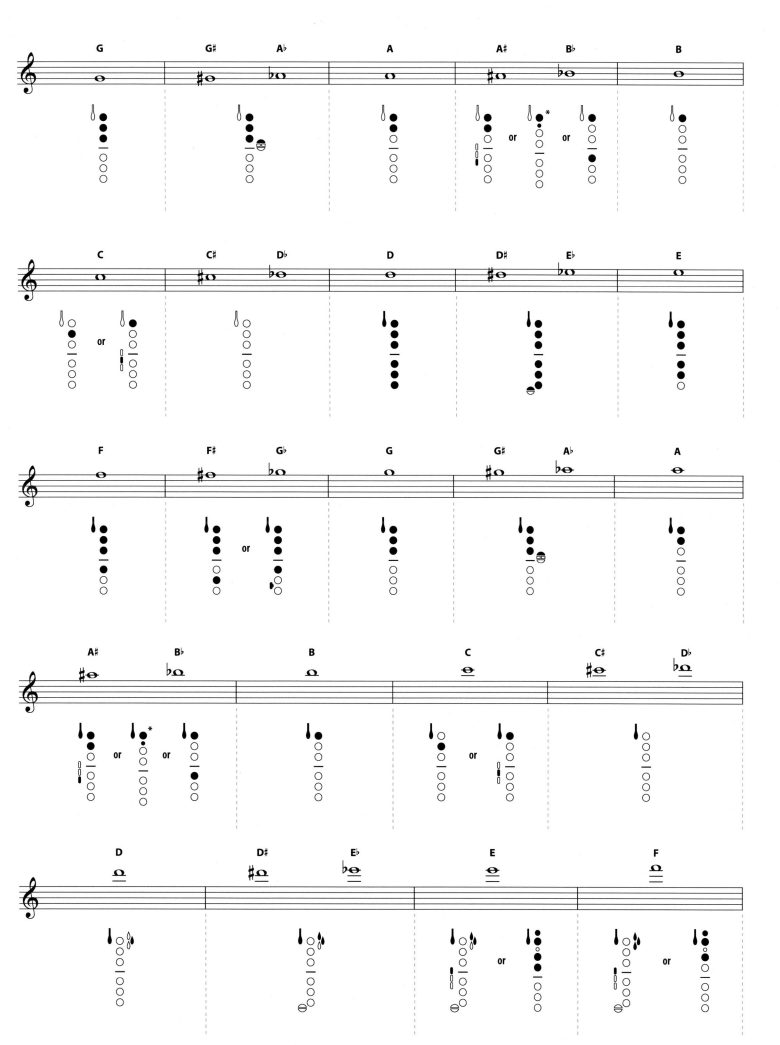

*The bis key is used for this fingering. This fingering should not be used in a chromatic scale.

Baritone Saxophone Fingering Chart

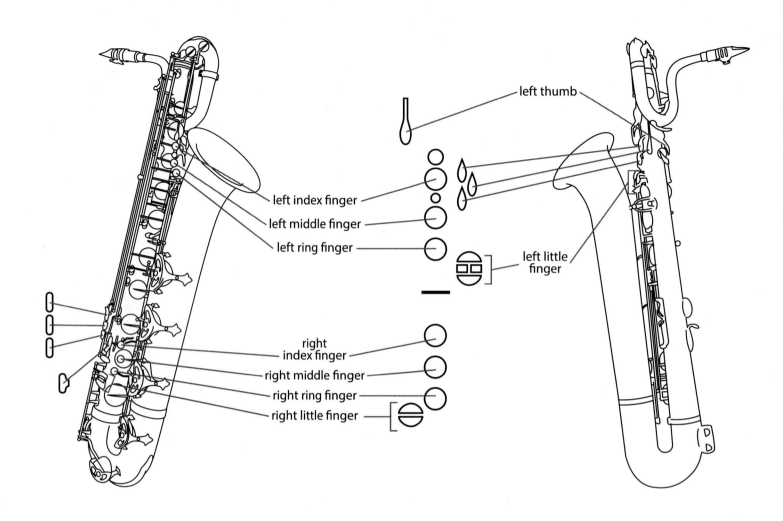

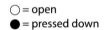

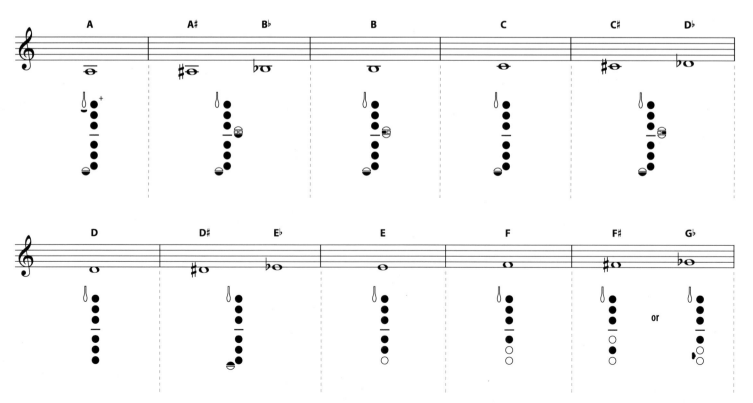

+This note is available on some baritone saxophone models.

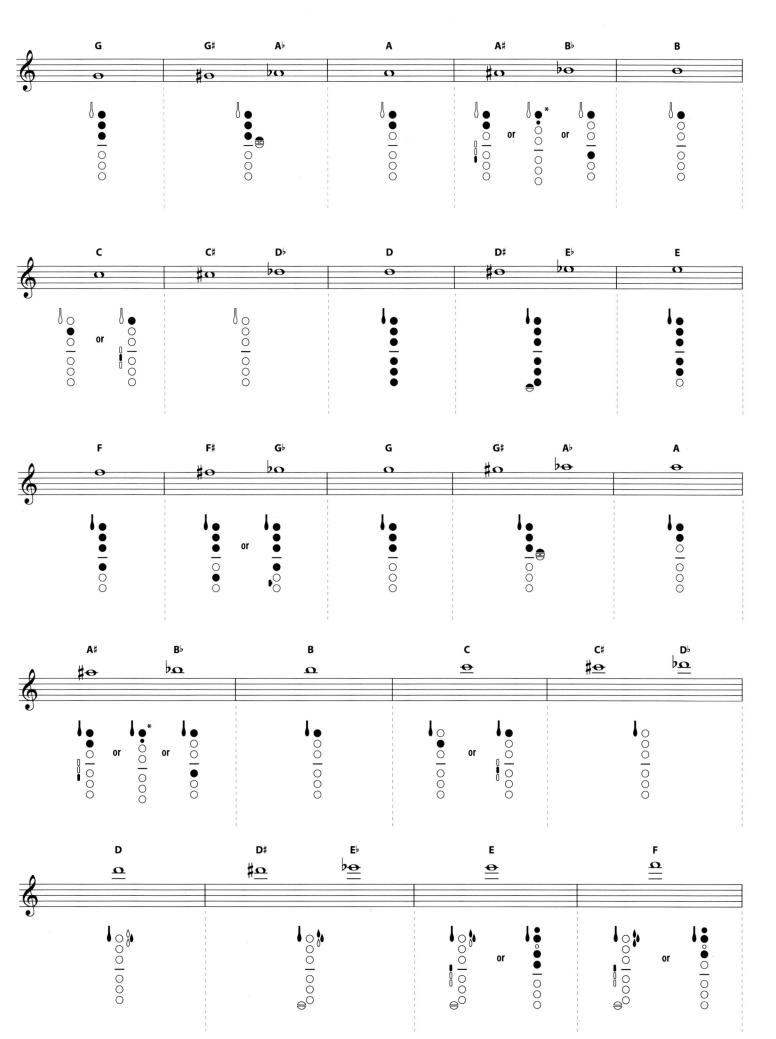

*The bis key is used for this fingering. This fingering should not be used in a chromatic scale.

Trumpet Fingering Chart

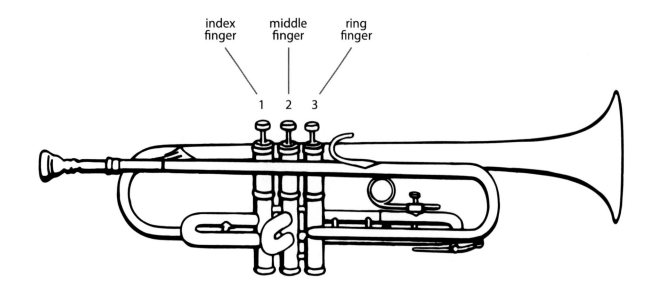

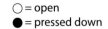

○ = open
● = pressed down

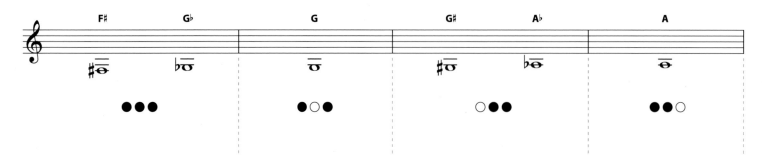

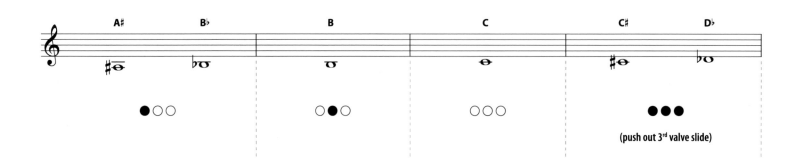

(push out 3rd valve slide)

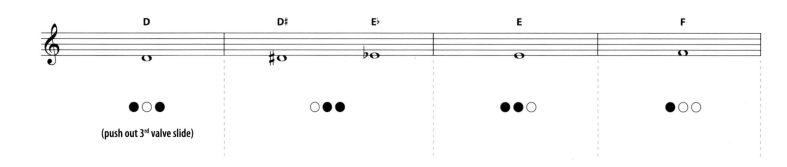

(push out 3rd valve slide)

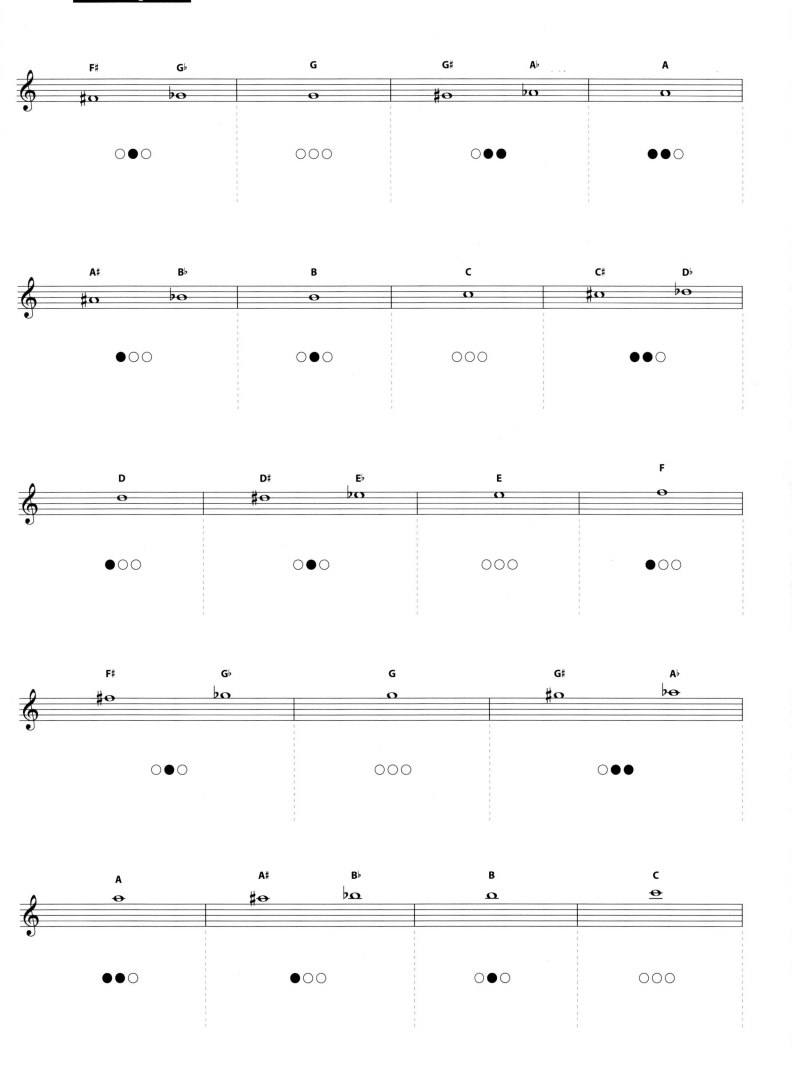

Horn in F Fingering Chart

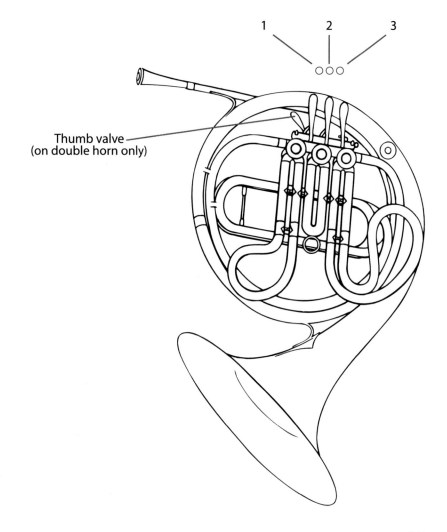

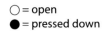
○ = open
● = pressed down

F Horns: Use the upper fingerings.
B♭ Horns: Use the lower fingerings.
The "T" only applies to double horns.

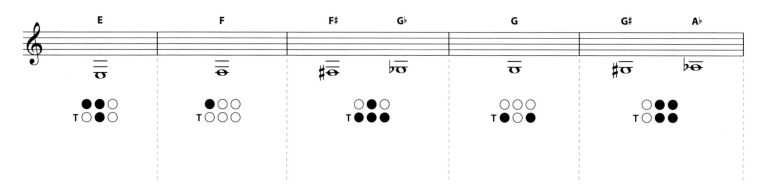

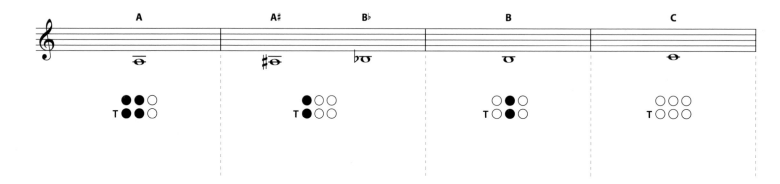

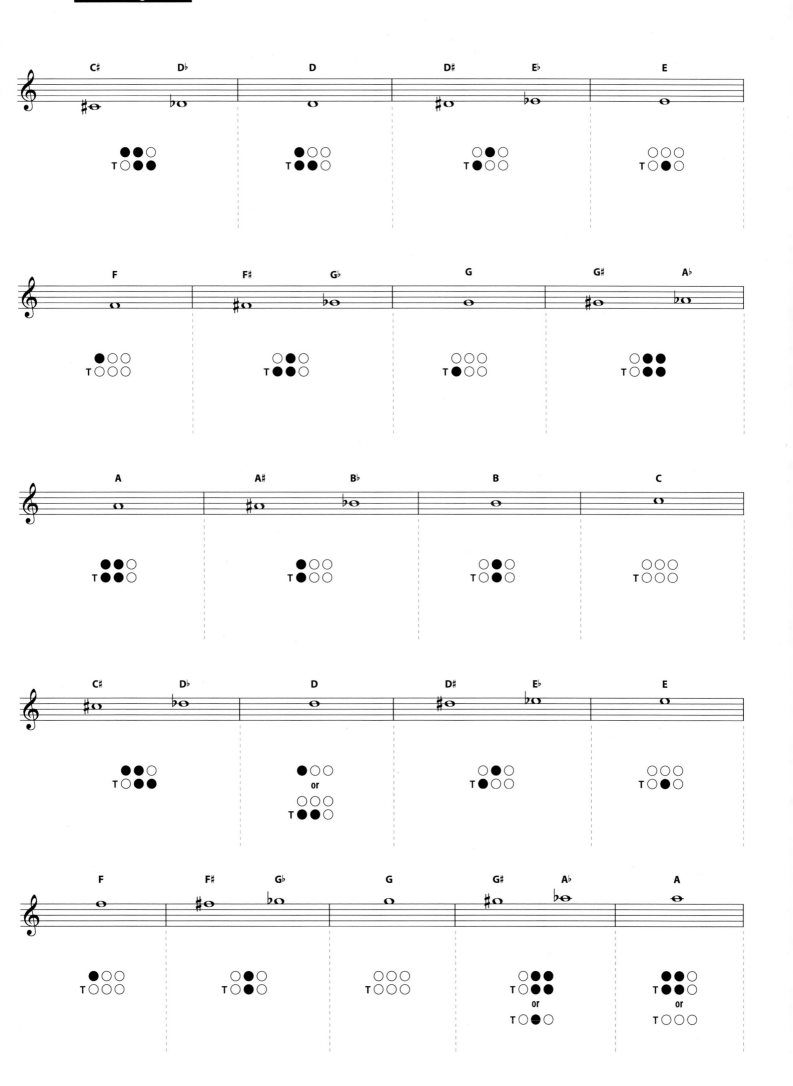

Trombone Slide Position Chart

This diagram indicates where the top of the slide is located in each position.

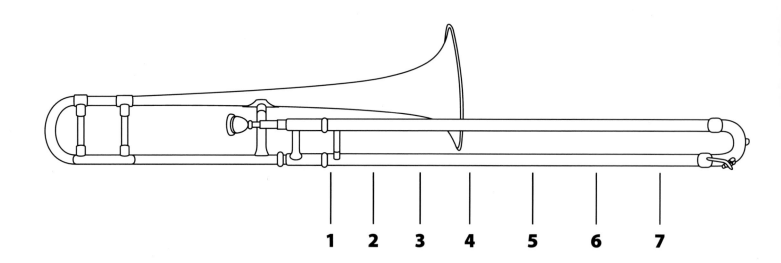

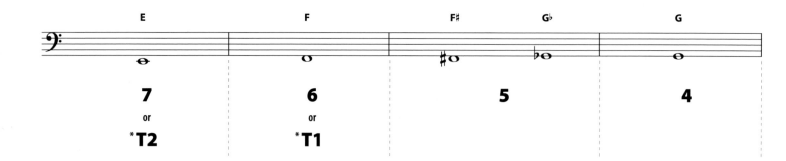

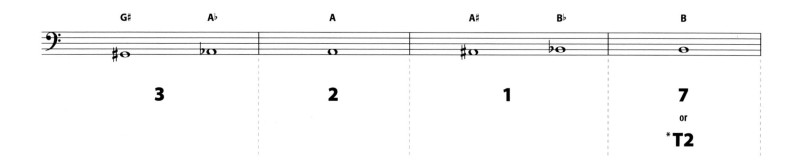

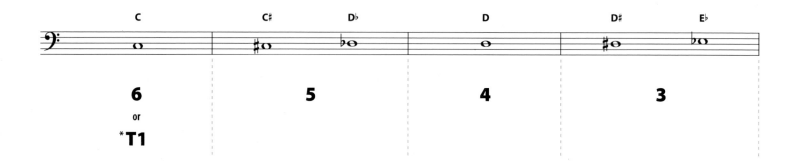

*If playing on an instrument with an F attachment, "T" slide positions should be used.

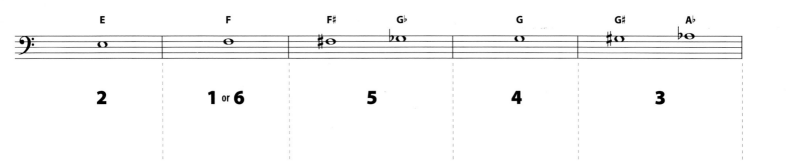

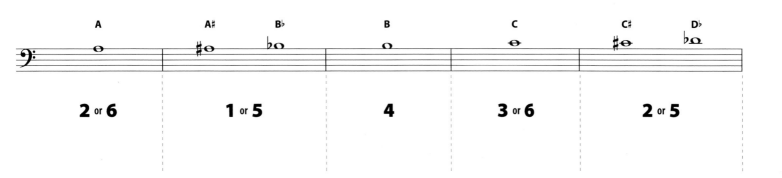

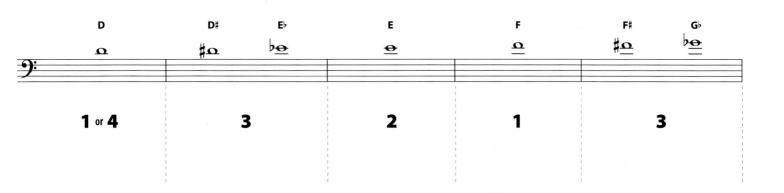

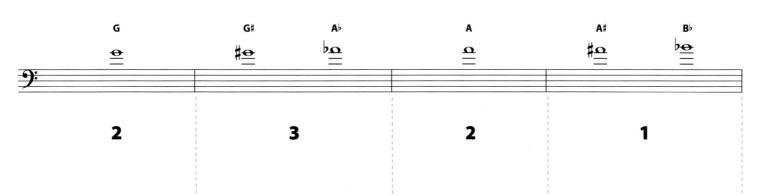

Baritone/Euphonium B.C. Fingering Chart

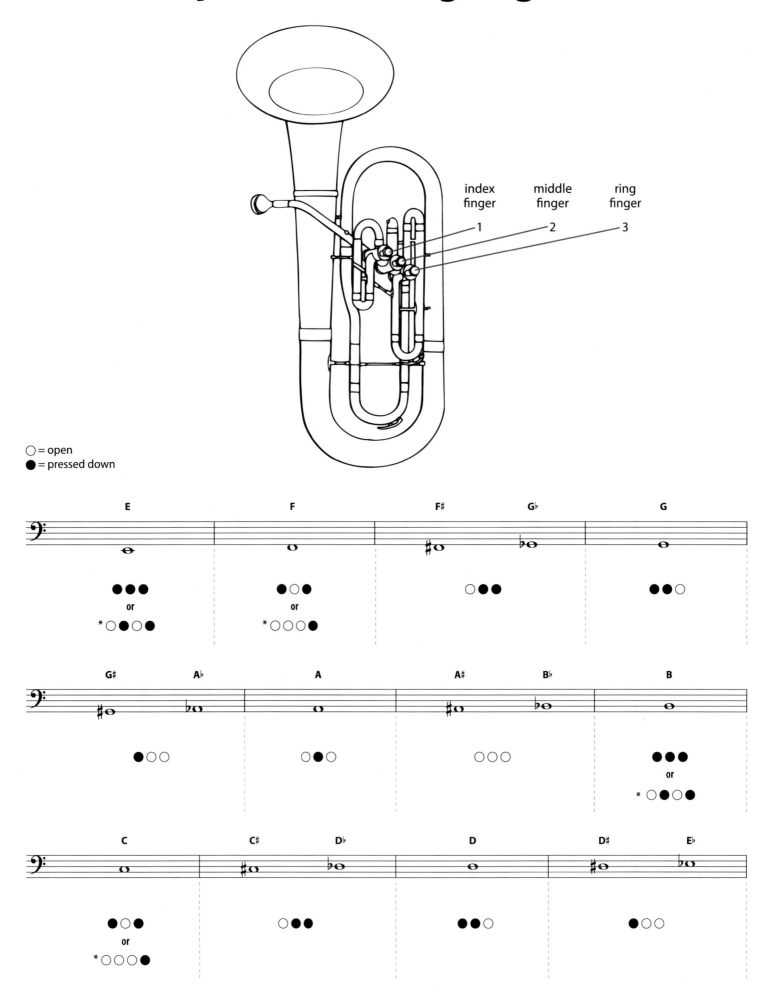

*If playing on an instrument with 4 valves, use the alternate fingering.

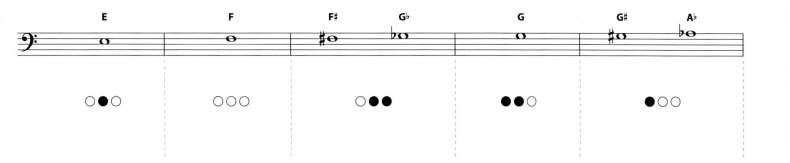

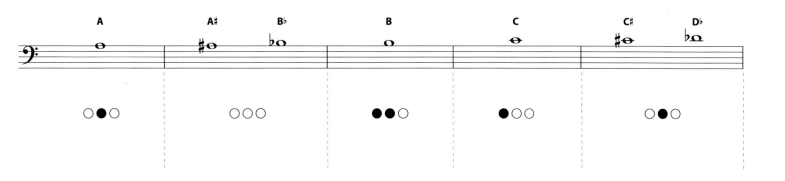

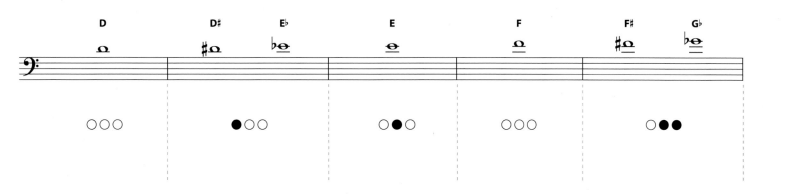

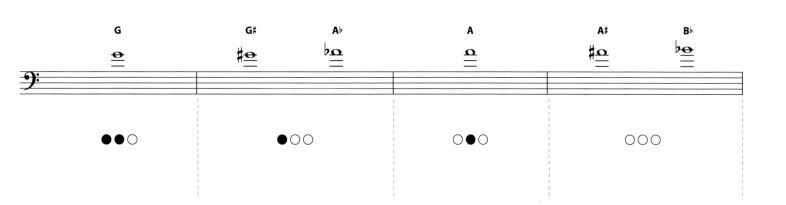

Baritone/Euphonium T.C. Fingering Chart

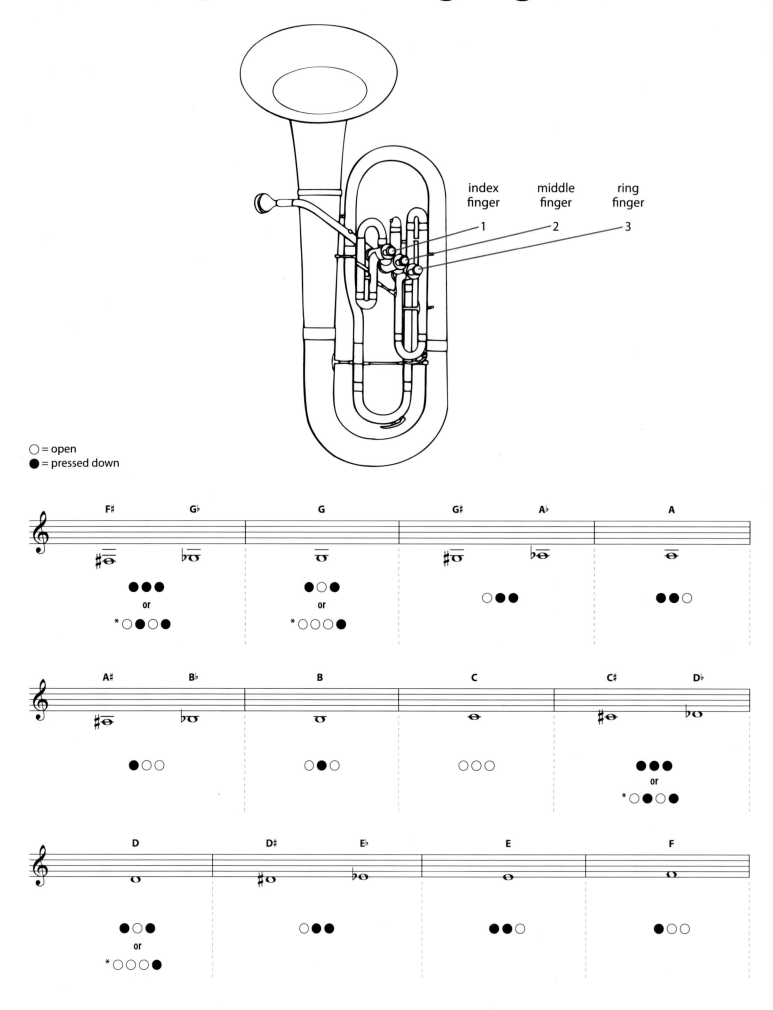

*If playing on an instrument with 4 valves, use the alternate fingering.

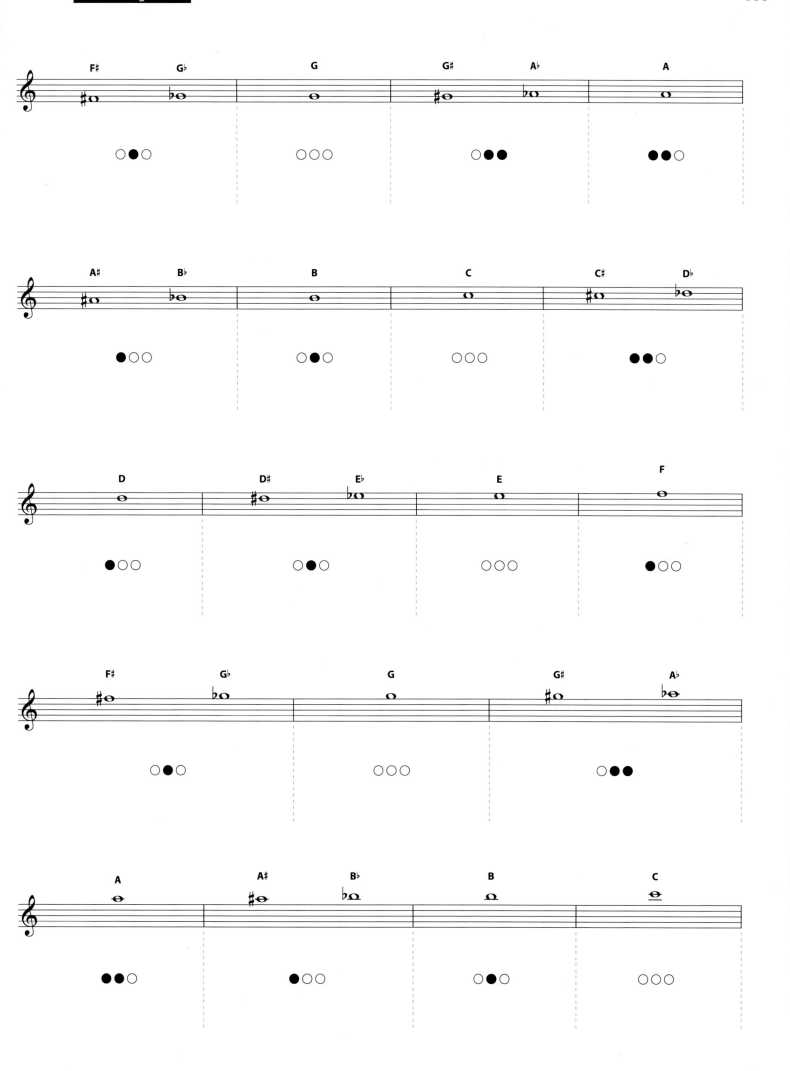

Electric Bass Fingering Chart

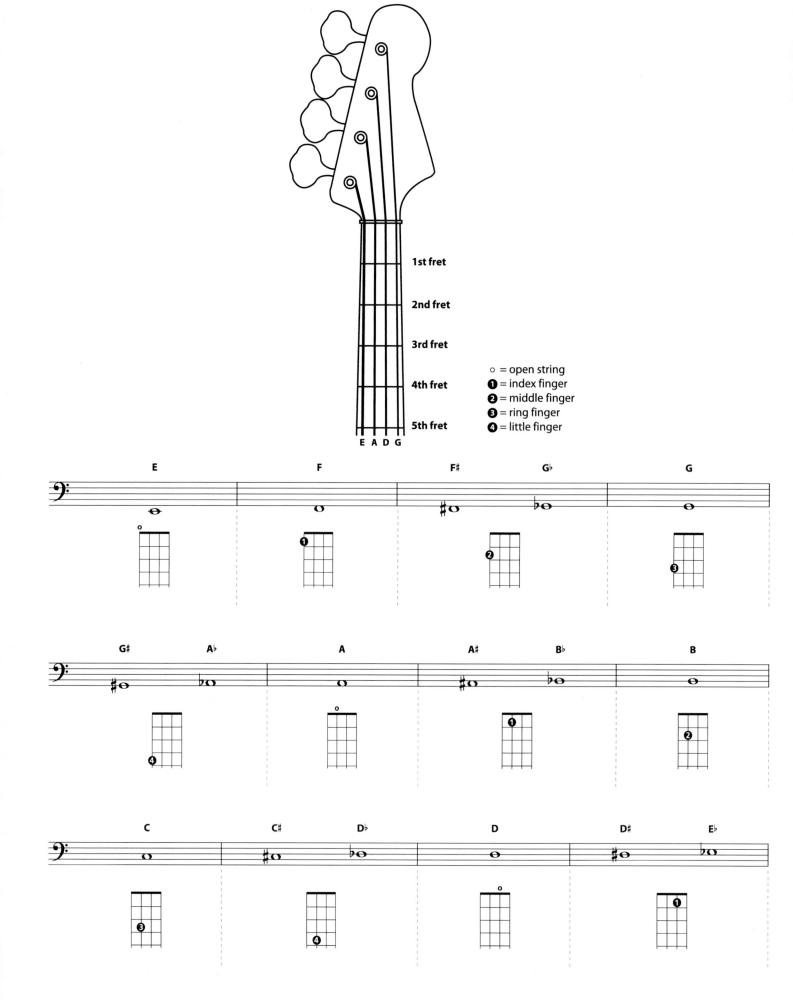

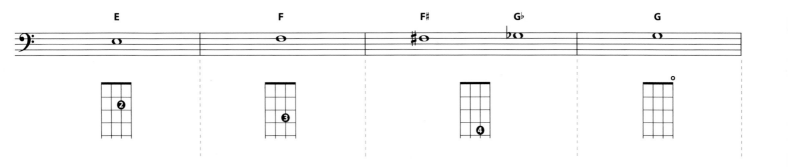

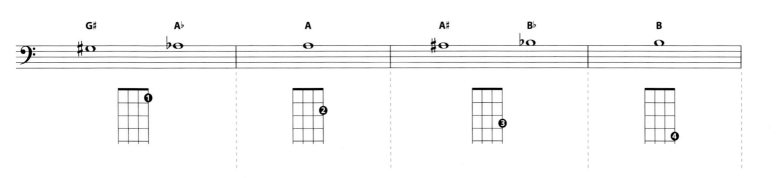

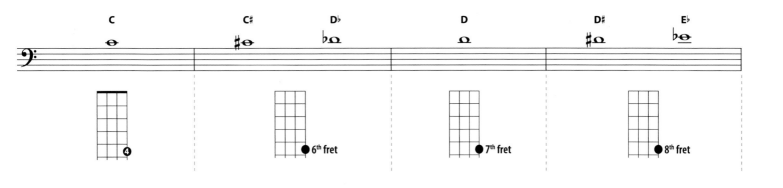

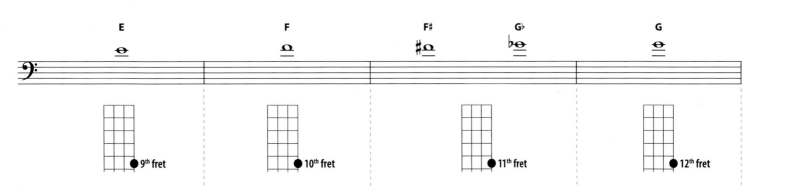

Tuba Fingering Chart

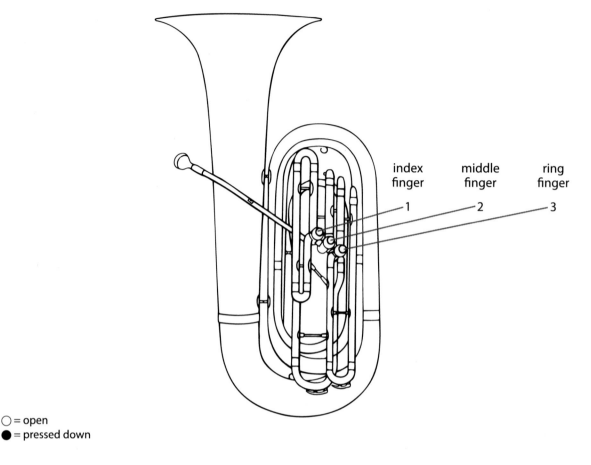

index finger   middle finger   ring finger

1   2   3

○ = open
● = pressed down

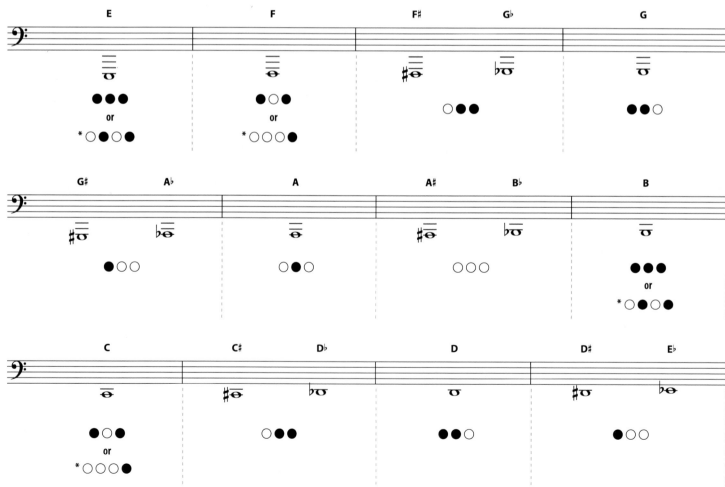

*If playing on an instrument with 4 valves, use the alternate fingering.

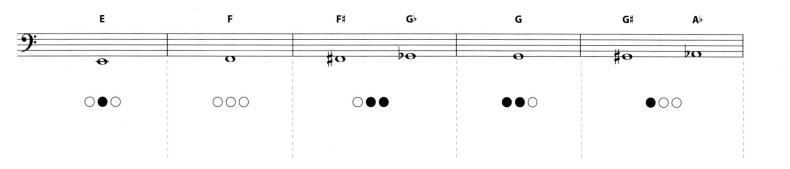

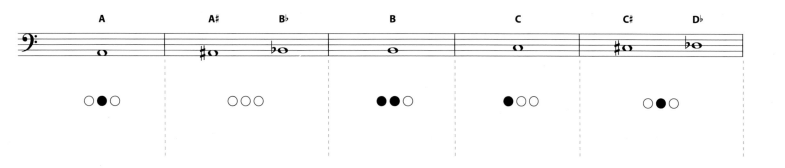

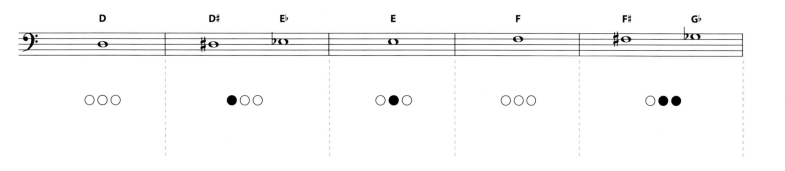

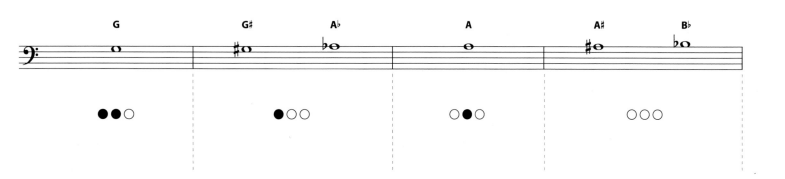

Mallet Percussion

YOUR INSTRUMENT–KEYBOARD (MALLET) PERCUSSION

The keyboard percussion family includes orchestra bells, xylophone, marimba, vibraphone and chimes.
Each instrument is arranged chromatically in two rows similar to a piano keyboard. Because of the different
materials used, each instrument has a unique sound. Since few of the keyboard percussion instruments
have been standardized in range, the most practical ranges for school use are listed below.

ORCHESTRA

BELLS (also called
Bells or Glockenspiel)
Although some
student bell kits
are 1 ½ octaves, the
standard range is 2½
octaves. The instrument
is played with brass,
plastic or hard-rubber mallets.

MARIMBA

The most
practical
range is
either a 4 or
4⅓ octave
instrument.
It is played
with yarn, cord-wound or rubber mallets.
Do not use wood, plastic or metal mallets!

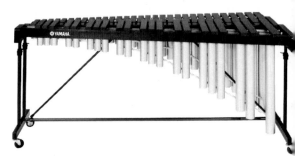

XYLOPHONE

The most practical range is either a 3 or 3½ octave
instrument. It is played with wood or hard-rubber mallets.
Do not use metal mallets!

CHIMES

(also called Tubular Bells)
The standard range for this
instrument is 1½ octaves. It is
played by striking the ridge of the
cap at the top of each tube with
a hammer-shaped mallet made of
rawhide. A foot-operated damper
pedal controls the sustain.

VIBRAPHONE (also called Vibraharp)

The standard range for this instrument is 3
octaves. It is played with yarn and cord-wound
mallets. Do not use brass mallets! A foot-
operated damper pedal controls the sustain.

CARE AND MAINTENANCE

A. Use a cloth to keep your mallet instruments clean.
The use of furniture polish on wooden bars should
be avoided as it will leave a residue. When not in
use, the instruments should be covered.

B. Mallets should be stored in a bag with your sticks.

C. Other than mallets, do not set anything on top of a
keyboard instrument. It is not a table!

BELLS

Bells sound two octaves higher than written.

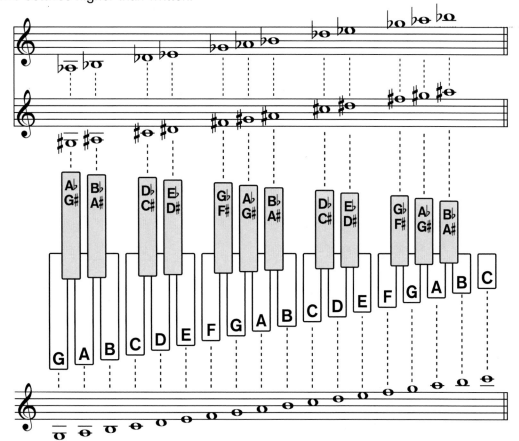

XYLOPHONE

The xylophone sounds one octave higher than written.

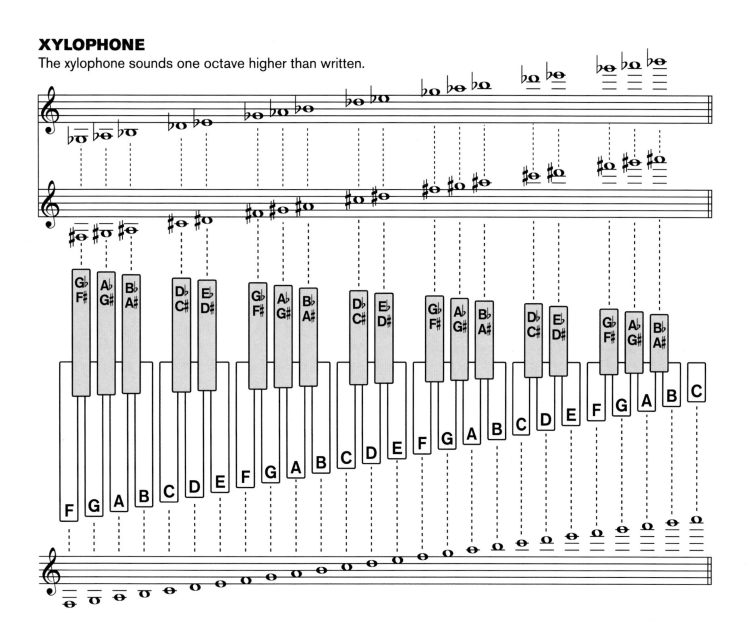

Percussive Arts Society International Drum Rudiments

All rudiments should be practiced: *open* (slow) to *close* (fast) to *open* (slow) and/or at an even, moderate march tempo.

I. ROLL RUDIMENTS

A. SINGLE STROKE ROLL RUDIMENTS

1. **Single Stroke Roll***

2. **Single Stroke Four**

3. **Single Stroke Seven**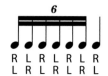

B. MULTIPLE BOUNCE ROLL RUDIMENTS

4. **Multiple Bounce Roll**

5. **Triple Stroke Roll**

C. DOUBLE STROKE OPEN ROLL RUDIMENTS

6. **Double Stroke Open Roll***

7. **Five Stroke Roll***

8. **Six Stroke Roll**

9. **Seven Stroke Roll***

10. **Nine Stroke Roll***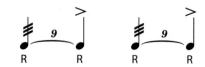

11. **Ten Stroke Roll***

12. **Eleven Stroke Roll***

13. **Thirteen Stroke Roll***

14. **Fifteen Stroke Roll***

15. **Seventeen Stroke Roll**

II. DIDDLE RUDIMENTS

16. **Single Paradiddle***

17. **Double Paradiddle***

18. **Triple Paradiddle**

19. **Single Paradiddle-Diddle**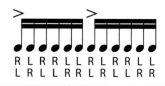

These rudiments are also included in the original Standard 26 American Drum Rudiments.

III. FLAM RUDIMENTS

20. Flam*

LR   RL

21. Flam Accent*

LR L R RL R L

22. Flam Tap

LR RRL LLR RRL L

23. Flamacue*

LR L R LLR
RL R L RRL

24. Flam Paradiddle*

LR L R RRL R L L

25. Single Flammed Mill

LR R L RRL L R L

26. Flam Paradiddle-Diddle*

LR L R R L LRL R L L R R

27. Pataflafla

LR L RRLLR L RRL

28. Swiss Army Triplet

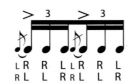

LR R LLR R L
RL L RRL L R

29. Inverted Flam Tap

LR LRL RLR LRL R

30. Flam Drag

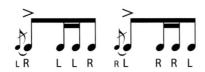

LR L L R RL R R L

IV. DRAG RUDIMENTS

31. Drag*

LLR   RRL

32. Single Drag Tap*

LLR L RRL R

33. Double Drag Tap*

LLRLLR LRRLRRL R

34. Lesson 25*

LLR L R LLR L R
RRL R L RRL R L

35. Single Dragadiddle

RR L R R LL R L L

36. Drag Paradiddle #1*

R LLR L R R L RRL R L L

37. Drag Paradiddle #2*

R LLR LLR L R R L RRL RRL R L L

38. Single Ratamacue*

LLR L R L RRL R L R

39. Double Ratamacue*

LLR LLR L R L RRL RRL R L R

40. Triple Ratamacue*

LLR LLR LLR L R L RRL RRL RRL R L R

Accessory Percussion Instruments

CRASH (HAND) CYMBALS

A. Start with a basic pair of sixteen- to eighteen-inch medium-weight cymbals.

B. Grasp the strap between the top of the first joint of the index finger and the flat, fleshy part of the thumb (close to the top of the bell). Do not put your hands through the loop of the straps.

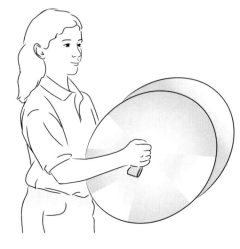

PLAYING THE CRASH CYMBALS

A. Hold the cymbals at approximately chest level.

B. For a right-handed player, keep the left cymbal stationary and strike the right cymbal against it with a glancing blow. The right cymbal should strike the left cymbal at an angle to avoid an air pocket. Once the crash has been executed, the cymbals should move apart so they can ring freely.

C. The distance between the cymbals will be wider for louder crashes and smaller for softer ones.

D. To muffle or choke the cymbals, draw them against your chest or forearms.

THE SUSPENDED CYMBAL

A suspended cymbal may be played with drumsticks or a variety of marimba and timpani mallets. Rhythmic

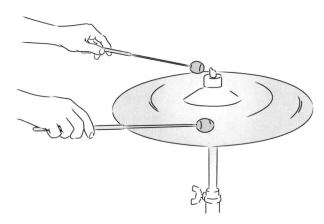

passages are best articulated with snare drum sticks played near the edge.

CARE AND MAINTENANCE

A. Fingerprints and dirt can be removed by using a solution of mild liquid detergent and warm water. Most cymbal manufactures also market specially formulated cymbal-cleaning products as well.

B. Never use steel wool, wire brushes or other abrasive cleansers.

THE WOODBLOCK

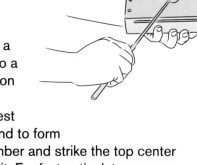

A. The woodblock may be played by holding it in the hand, mounted to a clamp (attached to a stand), or placed on a padded table. To produce the best tone, cup your hand to form a resonating chamber and strike the top center above the open slit. For fast, articulate passages, place the woodblock on a padded table and play it with two sticks or mallets.

B. It is most commonly played with medium-hard to hard rubber xylophone mallets. The tip or shoulder of a drumstick may also be used for more articulate passages.

THE TAMBOURINE

A. Hold the tambourine in one hand with your thumb placed on the head and your fingers wrapped around the shell. It should be held at least chest high and at a slight angle to the floor.

B. For soft, rapid passages, place the tambourine on a horizontal, towel-covered music stand or padded table, and play it with the fingertips, sticks or mallets.

THE TRIANGLE

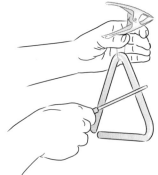

A The triangle is suspended from a triangle clip with a thin piece of nylon line. It can be held with the hand (at eye level), or attached to a music stand.

B. It is usually played with a steel beater and may be struck in a variety of spots, including the bottom or the side opposite the opening.

CLAVES

Claves should be held at chest level. Hold one clave in either hand (cupped to form a resonating chamber) and strike it sharply in the center with the clave in the opposite hand.

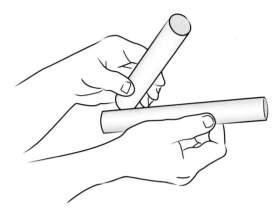

MARACAS

Maracas are held at chest level (parallel to the floor) and played using quick, downward wrist strokes. The index finger may be placed on top of the maraca to produce a more articulate stroke.

To play rolls, hold the maracas perpendicular to the floor and use fast, alternating wrist shakes.

COWBELL

The cowbell is held in the palm of the hand (either with the open end away from you or towards you) and struck with the butt-end of a stick or mallet held in the opposite hand. Depending on the desired sound, the cowbell can be struck on the upper topside or the open end (also referred to as the lip).

Strike the open end of the cowbell with the side of the stick.

Strike the top of the cowbell with the tip of the stick.

Timpani

THE PARTS OF THE TIMPANI

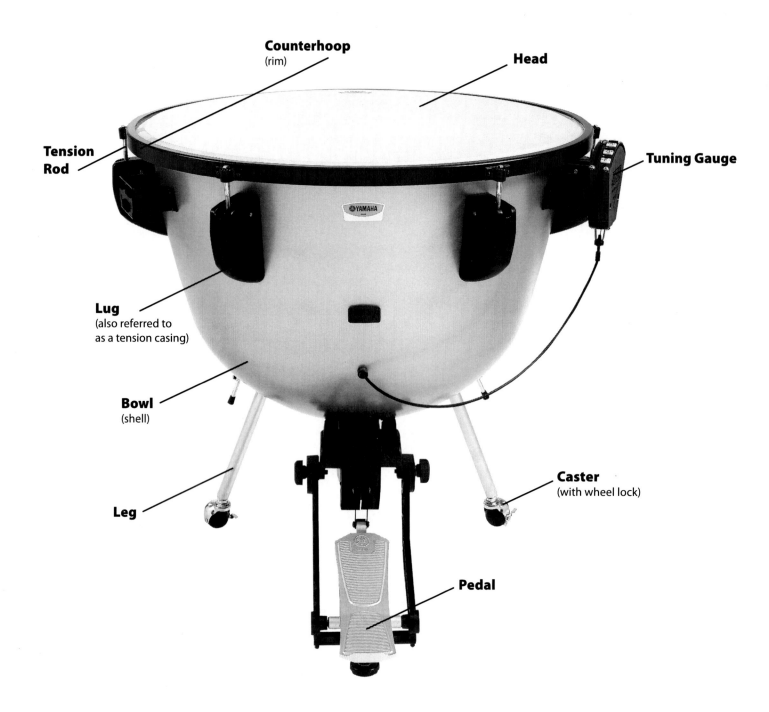

Counterhoop (rim)

Head

Tension Rod

Tuning Gauge

Lug (also referred to as a tension casing)

Bowl (shell)

Caster (with wheel lock)

Leg

Pedal

TIMPANI RANGES

With the pedals down to their lowest position, set the proper range of each drum by tuning the head to the following fundamental notes. When using only two drums, it is recommended you use the 26- and 29-inch drums.

32" = D   26" = B♭

29" = F   23" = D

INSTRUMENT PLACEMENT & PLAYING POSITION

Timpani are usually positioned so the lowest drum is to your left. If using more than two drums, arrange them in a semi-circle with the pedals facing you.

Stand behind the drums with your feet comfortably spread for proper balance and weight distribution. Some players prefer to lean against a stool to help facilitate pedal changes and to bring the arm position down to a comfortable playing position.

THE MALLET GRIP

The "German" grip, as opposed to the "French" grip, is often used by beginning players and is similar to the matched grip used for playing the snare drum. Let's review the matched grip:

A. First, extend your right hand as if you were going to shake hands with someone.

B. Place the mallet between your thumb and the first joint of your index finger, approximately ⅓ the way up from the end of the mallet.

C. Curve the other fingers around the shaft of the mallet.

D. Turn your hand over so your palm is facing towards the floor.

E. Repeat steps A–D with your left hand.

TUNING

Most beginning students start off matching the pitch from an external source such as a pitch pipe or keyboard percussion instrument. It is important to listen for pitch relationships within the ensemble (soloist, chord, etc.) and to check your tuning periodically.

STRIKING THE DRUM

Depending on the size of the drum, strike the head about 2 to 5 inches in from the bowl's edge making sure the heads of both mallets are side by side. To produce the best tone, the forearms should be relaxed and nearly parallel to the floor when the head is struck. Immediately following impact, the mallet should rebound without restriction.

ROLLS

The timpani roll is one of the most characteristic sounds of the instrument and is produced by using rapidly alternating single strokes. Rolls are notated in the same manner as those for snare drum.

MUFFLING/DAMPENING

In order to control the amount of sustain, it may be necessary to dampen/muffle the head. This can be accomplished by using the last two or three fingers of either hand to stop the vibration. Players will sometimes dampen a note simultaneously while striking another to avoid the mixture of the two sounds.

CARE & MAINTENANCE

When not in use, heads should be covered with fiberboard discs and mallets should be kept in a stick bag or case. When moving the instrument, lift the drum from the struts rather than the counterhoop. When rolling or moving the drums over a threshold, make sure you lift the pedal mechanism from the floor.

Acknowledgements

The authors would like to thank the following wonderful composers for sharing their talents:

Roland Barrett

Andrew Boysen, Jr.

Ralph Ford

Rossano Galante

Robert Sheldon

Todd Stalter

Randall Standridge

Michael Story

The authors would also like to thank the following for their contribution to, and support of this project:

John O'Reilly, Kirk Moss, Mandy DeShrage, Dominick Ferrara, Jeffrey Bittner, Dennis Aquilina, Amy Larkey-Emelianoff, Matthew Stratton, Edward Argenziano, Meredith Boyan, Mark Donellan, Thom Proctor, Jim Cochran, and Cristina Bernotas